Comparative Regulation, Economic Analysis, and Applications of Private Equity in the United States and European Union

Irini Liakopoulou

Comparative Regulation, Economic Analysis, and Applications of Private Equity in the United States and European Union

Irini Liakopoulou

Academica Press
London - Washington

Library of Congress Cataloging-in-Publication Data

Names: Liakopoulou, Irini, author.
Title: Comparative regulation, economic analysis, and applications of private equity in the united states and european union / Irini Liakopoulou
Description: Washington : Academica Press, 2020. | Includes references and index.
Identifiers: LCCN 2020938772 | ISBN 9781680530940 (hardcover)

Irini Liakopoulou is Professor of Finance at Oklahoma University and part-time Professor of Macroeconomics at Union College-NY.

Dedicated to Sofia and Dimitris

CONTENTS

INTRODUCTION[1]

It is estimated that the private equity sector has around € 2,936 billion of assets under management worldwide[2], so as to be a relevant factor in the modern financial world. Well, from the calculations it appears that at the end of June 2018 (last available data) the assets managed by private equity funds with a focus on Europe had reached € 1,620 billion from the 1,545 billion in December 2017, with a growth of 75 billion in deposits in six months[3].

From the growing interest in private equity and its potential, a copious (but often contradictory) literature has developed. The present work, divided into four chapters, intends to examine and systematically recompose some of the main issues dealt with by the economic literature and by the legal doctrine on private equity. The exam will be completed by observations drawn from international practice, recommendations and critical ideas for private equity operators, legislators and regulatory authorities. The ambition is to contribute to the deepening of technical knowledge on private equity. In light of the market potential and in the presence of a particularly fragile traditional system of business financing (banks and capital markets), the further development of the private equity sector could facilitate the flow of capital and other resources to companies, helping them to be more innovative, productive and competitive.

The first chapter of this work concerns the framework and context of private equity. The origin of private equity will be reconstructed, to then illustrate the evolution of the phenomenon in the United States and Europe. The dual function of private equity will then be analyzed, i.e. as

---

[1] The present work is updated until February 2020.

2 GLOBAL PRIVATE EQUITY REPORT 2019, Bain & Company, Boston, Massachusetts-USA, pp.7-8.

3 LUCIANO S., *"Cosa sono e perchè vanno molto bene i fondi di private equity,"* in Italia Oggi, n.164, 13/7/2019, p.4.

an investment opportunity for professional investors and as a financing tool for the real economy. The chapter will be completed with a brief description of the main investment techniques through private equity, including the acquisition of corporate control through debt (leveraged buy-out).

The second chapter focuses on the economic analysis of private equity. The reference economic model will be reconstructed, with particular attention to the detailed financial flows to and from the private equity firm and the private equity fund. This reconstruction will be instrumental for the subsequent analysis of the current remunerative policies and practices of private equity firms and the illustration of recommendations to improve these policies and practices, especially from the period of severe subprime crisis onwards. A critical reconstruction of the complex framework outlined by the literature on the issue of the economic impact of private equity and the alleged value creation will follow. The reconstruction will be completed by the presentation of an innovative thesis which relates private equity to the debt capital market (i.e. corporate finance).

The third chapter proposes the sectors where private equity can develop after the drastic drop in funding caused by the subprime crisis from 2007 onwards. The infrastructure sector in relation to environmental sustainability is the probable example of this attempt.

In the fourth chapter, the private equity regulatory frameworks in the United States and in the European Union will be reconstructed, analyzed and compared in order to highlight both the differences between the two systems and the deviations from the international agreements relating to the reform of the financial system. which the G20 leaders reached after the London summit in 2009.

Finally, taking into account the previous comparative regulatory analysis, possible future scenarios of the private equity market will be assumed. The work will end with critical points for operators, the European legislator and regulatory authorities, also drawn up in the light of the results of the economic analysis of private equity and comparative regulatory analysis.

CHAPTER 1
Introduction to the concept of private equity

1. Historical notes on private equity

The first medium/long-term investments in risk capital, similar to private equity operations, date back to the republican age of Rome. It is said that, in the time of Julius Caesar, the wealthy consul Marco Licinio Crasso invested venture capital in a fire service company in Rome (a sort of private firefighters, since there were no public firefighters at the time)[4].

However, the literature agrees that modern private equity only arose in 1946, when Georges F. Doriot (professor at Harvard Business School), Karl Compton (president of the Massachusetts Institute of Technology) and Ralph E. Flanders founded American Research and Development Corporation (ARDC) in Boston[5]. ARDC was a venture capital investment firm of companies that used war technologies developed for World War II[6]. The economic model of ARDC was simple

---

4 ANTONELLI G., *Crasso, il banchiere di Roma*, Rome, Italy, Newton, 1995. CASELLI S., *Private Equity and Venture Capital in Europe: Markets, Techniques, and Deals*, Oxford, Academic Press, 2010, pp. 3ss.

5 DE MARIA C., *Introduction to private equity,* Chichester, UK, John Wiley & Sons Ltd, 2010, pp. 20ss. LERNER J., *Venture Capital and Private Equity-A Casebook,* New York, USA, John Wiley & Sons Ltd., 1999. GUPTA U., *The First Venture Capitalist,* Calgary, Canada, Gondolier, 2004. WILSON J.W., *The New Venturers-Inside the High-Stakes Worls of Venture Capital,* Beverly, USA, Addison Wesley Publishing Company, 1986.

6 BARTLETT J., *Fundamentals of Venture Capital*, Lanham, USA, Madison Books, 1999, p.3: "According to Doriot, investments considered by [ARDC] involved: (1) New technology, new marketing concepts, and new product application possibilities; (2) a significant, although not necessarily controlling, participation by the investor in the company's management; (3) investment in ventures staffed by people of outstanding competence and integrity (herein the rule often referred to in venture capital as "bet the jockey, not the horse");(4) products or processes which have passed through at least the early prototype stage and are adequately protected by patents, copyrights, or trade-secrets agreements (the latter rule is often referred to as investing in situations where the information is "proprietary"); (5) situation which show promise

and successful: Investing in high-potential companies, providing capital and other resources with the aim of enhancing these companies and making a medium/long-term profit following the divestment from them. The success was fostered, in addition to the quality of the investments, by the lack of medium/long term financial resources for the development of the enterprises. Despite the success of its investments[7], ARDC did not survive the departure of Georges F. Doriot (in the early 70s), also due to the limitations of its legal architecture[8]. From the legal criticalities of ARDC, the limited partnership model for corporate venture capital investments developed, preferable to the corporate model for several reasons: First of all, the limited partnership separates the contributors of capital to be invested (limited partners) from the manager of the aforementioned capitals (general partner); moreover, the limited partnership has a predefined duration but does not prevent the general partner from continuing its management activities with reference to other limited partnerships; to the foregoing, it should be added that the limited partnership is generally "transparent" from a fiscal point of view (that is, profits are not taxed at the level of the limited partnership but at the higher level of its partners); finally, the distribution of profits to partners generally benefits from taxation with respect to the distribution of dividends to shareholders[9].

A series of regulatory interventions in the 1950s favored the development of the private equity market in the United States. In particular, in 1953 the Small Business Administration (SBA) was established, an authority that still exists today, the purpose of which is "to help, advise, assist and protect, as far as possible, the interests of small

---

to mature within few years to the point of an initial public offering or a sale of the entire company (commonly referred to as "exit strategy"); and (6) opportunities in which the venture capitalist can make a contribution beyond the capital dollars invested (often referred to as the "value-added strategy")."

7 Among the various successful investments, ARDC's investment in Digital Equipment Company is often mentioned, from which Compaq was subsequently formed, in turn merged by incorporation into Hewlett Packard.

8 HSU D. & KENNEDY M., *Organizing Venture Capital: the Rise and Demise of American Research & Development Corporation, 1946-1973*, in *Industrial and Corporate Change*, vol. 14, 2005, pp.579-616.

9 HARRIS L., *A Critical Theory of Private Equity*, in *Delaware Journal of Corporate Law*, vol. 35, 2010, 266 ss.

businesses"[10], also through the facilitated access to credit. The Small Business Investment Company Program (SBIC program) was established in 1958 to facilitate long-term capital inflow to small businesses that were unable to access credit through traditional channels (i.e., banks and capital markets)[11]. In particular, the Small Business Investment Company was able to access, through the SBA, subsidized loans aimed at making long-term investments in companies in the "start-up phase" (that is, in the early stages of the business cycle). The SBIC program, also thanks to tax incentives, was one of the main resources for the initial growth of the private equity market in the United States.

In the late 1970s, the US legislator allowed pension funds to make, albeit only partially, high-risk, high-yield investments (such as investments in private equity funds) thus favoring the financing of private equity[12]. Kohlberg Kravis Robert LP[13] was founded in the 1970s and contributed to the growth of the private equity market by developing an innovative technique of purchasing corporate control through debt: The so-called leveraged buy out[14].

---

10 U.S. Small Business Act of 30 July 1953, Sec. 2 (a), provides that: "It is the declared policy of the Congress that the government should aid, counsel, assist, and protect, insofar as is possible, the interests of small-business concerns."

11 CENDROWSKI H., MARTIN J., PETRO L., WADECKI A., *Private Equity: History, Governance and Operations*, Chichester, UK, John Wiley & Sons, 2008.

12 DE MARIA C., *Introduction to private equity*, op.cit., p.21.

13 BAKER G. P. & SMITH G. D., *The New Financial Capitalists – Kohlberg Kravis Roberts and the Creation of Corporate Value*, Cambridge, UK, Cambridge University Press, 1998. BRIGHAM E.F., HOUSTON J.F., *Fundamentals of Financial Management,* South-Western Pub, Concise Edition, 2019.

14 This procedure consists of a complex series of financial transactions aimed at purchasing a company. Usually, however, private equity firms are promoting this type of offer. The leveraged buy-out involves the creation of a special purpose vehicle (newco) in which the offeror's financial resources flow: Equity (capital) and debt (leveraged). In the next phase, the newco transfers the assets to the target company and then receives equity investments in the target company (less frequent event) or it can proceed with a merger by incorporation with the target company (more frequent event), generally resulting in the incorporated company. The contracted debt is then repaid either with the cash flows generated by the acquired company or by selling company branches or non-strategic assets. An essential requirement is that the target company is characterized by a low degree of leverage and a high ability to produce cash flow, precisely because the new company, born precisely from the incorporation, will have to be able to repay the debts covered by the acquisition.

Since the 1980s, the private equity market in the United States has seen periods of strong expansion[15] with sudden contractions[16], normally related to the performance of international financial markets. The literature agrees in observing that the US private equity market remains, to date, the most developed market both in terms of maturity and size, and for this reason, in the rest of the discussion it will be the reference model.

As for the European private equity market, the first institutional acts relating to its formation and development date back to the 1980s when the European Council sponsored the creation of the Venture Capital Liaison Office (a liaison office between private equity operators and European institutions) and when the European Venture Capital Association was created[17].

In these years, the European market was estimated to be about a quarter of a century behind the US market. And this is because there are strong differences in the development of private equity in the various countries, with the most developed Anglo-Saxon countries, with higher investment cuts on mature sectors, and with the Mediterranean European countries more concentrated on the small investment cut. Beyond geographical differences, these operators bring economic resources, technical managerial skills, and a strong network of contacts in high-potential companies that go through the most delicate phases of their life cycle.

Today, although the gap between the two markets has narrowed, the European private equity market still appears underdeveloped compared to the US market: With reference to the period 2014-2018, private equity investments in Europe reached 97.3 billion Euro and in the United States the 144.52 billion euros, i.e. the European countries have

---

15 The prosperity of the US market in the 1980s and the "battle" of the KKR fund for the acquisition of control of RJR Nabisco are abundantly described in BURROUGH B. & HELYAR J., *Barbarians at the Gate – The Fall of RJR Nabisco*, New York, USA, HarperCollins Publishers, 2008.

16 For example, the explosion of the "dot-com" bubble in 2000-2001 and, more recently, the "sub-prime" mortgage crisis in 2007-2008.

17 GERVASONI A. & SATTIN F. L., *Private equity e venture capital – Manuale di investimento nel capitale di rischio*, Milan, Italy, Guerini Studio, 2008, p.33. BYGRAVE W. D., HAY M. & PEETERS J.B., *Realizing Investment Value*, London, UK, Pitman Publishing, 1994.

invested 1/5 compared to that of the US. Moreover, ongoing political uncertainty in Europe has led to a drop in private equity deal making in 2019[18]. It is also noted that within the European Union individual national markets are highly fragmented: The relationship between private equity investments and domestic product gross in Italy is 0.09%, equal to about 1/3 of the corresponding ratio for the area of the European Union (0.26%) and significantly lower than the ratio for Germany, respectively (0.20%) , France (0.30%) and the United Kingdom (0.67%)[19].

With regard to private equity regulatory interventions, the European legislator intervened only recently - and in the context of the review of the financial system following the 2007-2008 crisis - through Directive 2011/61/EU (hereinafter, "AIFM Directive") relating to managers of alternative investment funds. This is obviously a first step towards creating a single market for financial services. It should be noted, however, that harmonization by means of a directive has as its limit the coexistence of the regime envisaged by the directive with the national regimes of transposition of the same which, among other things, is subject to sanctioning discipline[20].

The 2007-2008 "sub-prime" mortgage crisis prompted G20 leaders to rethink and reform the global financial system, including the private equity sector, and from that reform push it developed in the United States and the European Union a complex regulatory framework, which

---

18 Dominick Mondesir, private capital analyst for EMEA at PitchBook affirmed that: "Gps are opting for a wait and see approach as the risk of a hard Brexit has grown as of late. Only 12 mega-deals were completed in private equity in 2019, with 26 completed in 2018, demonstrating GP's increasingly cautious approach to writing bigger cheques for companies exposed to European political risk." 2019 ANNUAL REPORT, European PE Breakdown, PitchBook, 2020.

19 SZMIGIERA M., *Private equity-Statistics & Facts,* Statista, 2019.

20 For the sake of completeness, it should be noted that the European legislator is continuing on the path of creating a single market for financial services in the European Union with the approval of regulations, i.e. normative acts having a general scope and directly applicable in the laws of the Member States, regarding venture capital (see Regulation (EU) of the European Parliament and of the Council n. 345/2013 of 17 April 2013) and European funds for social entrepreneurship (see Regulation (EU) of the European Parliament and of the Council n. 346/2013 of 17 April 2013) as well as on long-term European investment funds (see proposal for a regulation of the European Parliament and of the Council SWD (2013) 230 and SWD (2013) 231), the discussion of which is outside the scope of this work .

entered into force only recently, which will be analyzed in the continuation of this work.

2. Definition of private equity

Although there is no universally accepted definition of private equity, we will use the proposed definition of US Legal which considers private equity as "a source of investment capital from wealthy individuals and institutions for the purpose of investing and acquiring equity ownership in companies. It is a type of investment in some asset in companies that are not publicly traded on a stock exchange. This type of investment is aimed at gaining significant, or even complete, control of a company in the hopes of earning a high return. The investment are made directly into private companies or there can be buyouts of public companies that result in a delisting of public equity. Generally, shares issued are proportional to the amount of the investment so that the person who has invested the majority of the money in effect controls the company."

Private equity is therefore an investment technique. For greater clarity, it seems useful to describe its main characteristics. The first characteristic concerns the object of the investment: These are generally equity investments (or financial instruments convertible into equity investments) of unlisted companies[21]. In particular, these are companies with high potential (in consideration of their management, market, products or services or, simply, the underestimation by the market or the subjects that control them), such as to justify a expectation of high return on investment for the private equity fund (and, therefore, for investors in the fund who bring financial resources to it). The second characteristic is the time horizon of private equity investments: Normally between three

---

21 LEVIN. J. S. & ROCAP D. E., *Structuring Venture Capital, Private Equity, and Entrepreneurial Transactions*, New York, USA, Wolters Kluwer Law & Business, 2013, p.103. In cases where the private equity investment relates to listed financial instruments, the initial objective is generally the revocation of the listing, followed by a phase of reorganization aimed at enhancing the business and subsequently divesting. For the sake of completeness, it is noted that the listing of financial instruments of companies subject to private equity investments is, generally, one of the methods of divestment by private equity operators, therefore it is the arrival point and not the starting point of the operations of private equity.

and seven years (also in consideration of the life cycle, usually between ten and thirteen years, of a private equity fund)[22]. The third characteristic regards the impact on the corporate governance of the company being invested: The private equity fund is usually represented in the management body of the company being invested in private equity (called the "portfolio company" because it becomes part of the "investment portfolio" of the private equity fund) to be able to monitor and direct its management. The fourth characteristic concerns the type of investors in the private equity fund (and therefore private equity lenders): They are typically professional investors, such as pension funds, insurance companies, banks, funds of funds, sovereign wealth funds and other qualified investors. The fifth characteristic concerns the contribution, by the private equity fund, not only of capital, but also of other resources (for example, management skills, greater international visibility and strategic opportunities) for the enhancement of the portfolio company; it is precisely this mixed contribution of resources (fungible and otherwise) that allegedly contributes to the creation of value through private equity investments[23].

It seems appropriate to clarify the meaning of the term private equity to distinguish it from two terms that are often confused with it: Venture capital and hedge funds.

Venture capital: The corporate doctrine identifies two macro-phases relating to the life cycle of a company. The "start-up phase," that is, the first stages of the company's life and the complex of "post-start phases." Venture capital (literally "venture capital") is a particular category of private equity and properly refers to the contribution of capital and other resources to the company in its "start-up phase." According to this reconstruction, private equity includes venture capital (the latter being in declination)[24].

---

22 On the average duration and timing of private equity investments see: STRÖMBERG P., *The new demography of private equity*, in *The Global Impact of Private Equity Report 2008 – Globalization of Alternative Investments – Working Papers* (ed. by Lerner J. & Gurung A.), vol. 1, Geneva, Switzerland, World Economic Forum, 2008, p.3 ss.

23 DAMIANI E., *Venture Capital e Private Equity*, Naples, Italia, Edizioni Scientifiche Italiane, 2010, p.13 ss.

24 For completeness, it is noted that some scholars do not consider venture capital as a category of private equity, but as an investment technique independent of private

Hedge funds: The term means a speculative investment fund that usually invests in listed financial instruments (unlike private equity investments which are normally in unlisted financial instruments), whose time horizon is generally short-term (unlike of private equity investments whose time horizon is medium to long term) and with the possibility for investors to request the repayment of their share in the investment fund at any time or at predetermined intervals (unlike private equity investors the whose share in the fund is generally illiquid and non-transferable). In addition, hedge funds (unlike private equity funds) often make use of investment strategies that include the use of financial derivative instruments or other complex financial instruments. Both hedge funds and private equity funds make use of third party loans (leverage), with the difference that in private equity investments only their own portfolio company is indebted to the third party creditor (and therefore only the portfolio company is exposed insolvency and bankruptcy in the event of non-repayment of the loan in question). However, the distinction between private equity investments and hedge fund investments is less and less marked, because there is a progressive evolution of the hedge fund market (which is increasingly overlapping with the products and services of the private equity market) and both private equity investments that hedge fund investments are now subject to the same regulatory framework[25].

3. Value chain, cycle and function of private equity

To understand the functioning and dynamics of private equity it is necessary to briefly illustrate the context, the value chain and the phases

---

equity. According to this reconstruction, venture capital deals exclusively with the needs of the company in the start-up phase, while private equity deals with the needs of the company in all the other phases subsequent to the start-up phase, on the point see: CASELLI S., *Private Equity and Venture Capital in Europe: Markets, Techniques, and Deals*,Oxford, UK, Academic Press, 2010, p.4 ss.

25 For further details see: MCCAHERY J. A. & VERMEULEN E. P. M., *The Contractual Structure and Regulation of Private Equity Funds and Hedge Funds*, in *LSE Working Paper*, n. 50/2008, 2008, p.6 ss., http://www.lse.ac.uk/fmg/research/RICAFE/pdf/RICAFE2-WP50-McCahery.pdf.GILLIGAN J. & WRIGHT M., *Private Equity Demistified: An Explanatory Guide*, London,UK, The Institute of Chartered Accountants in England and Wales, 2008, p. 23 ss.. GILLIGAN J. & WRIGHT M., *Private Equity Demistified: 2012 Update*, London, UK, The Institute of Chartered Accountants in England and Wales, 2012.

that mark the private equity cycle, as well as the function of private equity in the business cycle.

In international practice, private equity transactions are carried out through an investment fund in private and venture capital of companies (for the sake of brevity, "private equity fund" or "fund") managed indirectly by a private equity firm. Typically, the private equity fund is organized in the form of a limited partnership (or other functionally equivalent legal structure)[26] and managed externally by a private equity firm. The private equity firm (think, for example, of Texas Pacific Group[27], Bain Capital[28] or Warburg Pincus[29]) is the vehicle, usually with a shareholder base or established in the form of a partnership, in which professionals and specialists of private equity[30] come together. Within the framework of private equity, there are three main groups of subjects: a) Private equity firm and subjects affiliated or attributable to it. The private equity firm delegates the management of one or more funds to some of its professionals, called sponsors. The latters have the task, first, to capitalize the fund by collecting commitments and financial resources from investors and, then, to identify, select and make investments in high potential companies. Their goal is to enhance these companies and generate profits for the fund (that is, for investors in the fund) by divesting them from these companies in the medium/long term. b) Investors in the private equity fund: These are typically professional investors such as pension funds, insurance companies, banks, funds of funds, sovereign wealth funds and other qualified investors who, in turn, invest capital entrusted to them by

---

26 PERSAUD A. & ATKINSON A., *Private Equity Funds: Legal Analysis of Structural, ERISA, Securities and Other Regulatory Issues*, in *Investment Adviser Regulation* (ed. by di Kirsch E. K.), New York, USA, Practising Law Institute, 2012, §47:2:1.

27 For institutional information on Texas Pacific Group, see https://tpg.com/.

28 For institutional information on Bain Capital, see: http://www.baincapital.com/.

29 For institutional information on Warburg Pincus, see: http://www.warburgpincus.com/.

30 For completeness, it is noted that some private equity firms have applied for admission to trading of their securities on regulated markets, for example Blackstone Group L.P. o 3i Group plc. The discussion of the peculiarities of listed private equity firms is beyond the scope of this work, but for further details see: BERGMANN B., CHRISTOPHERS H., HUSS M. & ZIMMERMANN H., *Listed Private Equity*, in *Private Equity: Fund Types, Risks and Returns, and Regulation* (ed. by Cumming D. J.), Hoboken, USA, John Wiley & Sons, 2009, pp.53-70.

the market (the subjective characteristics of the investors in private equity funds-in particular, their level of experience and knowledge in high risk/yield investments, such as private equity - allows private equity firms to operate under a private placement scheme, a less onerous regime compared to the public one or with retail investors)[31]. c) Portfolio companies: High-potential companies looking for medium/long-term capital and other resources for the development of their business or underestimated by the market or by those who control it before the intervention of a private equity fund.

For the sake of completeness, it is noted that in the leveraged buy-out operations there are also third party external lenders (for example banks) that provide debt capital to the corporate vehicle created for the acquisition of control of a portfolio company.

The life cycle of a private equity fund coincides with the time horizon of the investment made by investors in this private equity fund and is typically between ten and thirteen years. In particular, the life of a fund is divided into five main phases[32]:

1) T0 (initial moment)-capital raising/fund creation: The sponsors invite potential investors to subscribe shares in the private equity fund. An illustrative document called a private placement memorandum is usually prepared to illustrate the characteristics and investment policies of the newly created fund. The private equity fund and the related corporate vehicles are established and final agreements with investors are signed[33].

2) T1 (typically within 5 years from T0)-investments in portfolio companies: After identifying and selecting investment opportunities, the private equity fund invites its investors to bring the subscribed capital within a short term (usually 10-15 days from the request) and, thanks to this financial funding, makes investments in portfolio companies[34].

---

31 GILLIGAN J. & WRIGHT M., *Private Equity Demistified: An Explanatory Guide*, London, UK, The Institute of Chartered Accountants in England and Wales, 2008, p.2 ss.

32 GERVASONI A. & SATTIN F. L., *Private equity e venture capital*, op.cit., p.483 ss.

33 NAIDECH S. W., *Private Equity Fund Formation*, New York, USA, Practical Law Company, 2011, p. 10 ss.

34 *Ibidem.*

3) T2 (between T1 and T3)-monitoring and enhancement of the portfolio companies: The private equity fund monitors and directs the performance of its portfolio companies and brings its skills with the aim of promoting development and increasing the value of portfolio company in view of divestment[35].

4) T3 (typically within 10 years from T0)-divestment from portfolio companies: The private equity fund divests from portfolio companies, that is, it sells investments in portfolio companies to third parties. In the event of a positive intervention, it realizes a capital gain on the investment[36].

5) T4 (typically within 10/13 years from T0)-fund/distribution closure: The private equity fund distributes the proceeds deriving from its investment and divestment activities, liquidating, distributing in kind or zeroing (accounting) the value of the investments in portfolio companies from which it was not possible to divest in good time[37].

The investment (T1), monitoring (T2) and divestment (T3) phases can, in turn, be divided into eight sub-phases:

1) Preliminary analysis: The private equity fund seeks, identifies and selects investment opportunities also thanks to reports from financial advisors, legal advisors, banks or other operators. The fund and the potential portfolio company enter into preliminary agreements (for example, confidentiality agreements and exclusive agreements with reference to the investment opportunity). They also exchange preliminary information relating to the investment opportunity.

2) Evaluation of investment opportunities: The fund analyzes the investment opportunity, creating a financial model in which, among other things, the expected growth of the potential portfolio company and the possibilities and timing related to the divestment are taken into consideration. The fund determines a price/amount fork to invest in the potential portfolio company.

3)Negotiation: A letter of intent - generally descriptive and non-binding - concerning the investment opportunity is signed. The exchange

35 *Ibidem.*
36 *Ibidem.*
37 *Ibidem.*

of information between the fund and the potential portfolio company continues, especially in the context of the analysis and technical checks (due diligence) by the fund and its consultants. Negotiation of the investment contract and related agreements begins (for example, the loan agreement, in the event that the investment is made through debt; the guarantee contracts; the shareholders' agreement in the event that the opportunity to investment does not concern the acquisition of a 100% investment; the incentive plans of the portfolio company management).

4) Structuring: The legal architecture by which the fund intends to realize the investment opportunity in the potential portfolio company is defined, taking into account, above all, the tax implications at the time of investment and at the time of divestment. Furthermore, the corporate governance of the potential portfolio company is clarified following the realization of the investment opportunity, so that the fund can adequately monitor and direct its management.

5) Further analysis and verifications: This phase continues until the signing of the definitive agreements but can extend even further (in the latter case, the definitive agreements are usually conditioned by the positive outcome of technical checks to be carried out between the signing of the agreements and the improvement of the same).

6) Signing and closing: The investment agreements (signing) and execution of the same are signed, respectively, so that the investment (closing) of the private equity fund in the portfolio company can be completed.

7) Monitoring: The fund monitors the performance and results of the portfolio company both in terms of control and in terms of direction. The fund also begins to identify and plan divestment opportunities aimed at maximizing its return on investment in the portfolio company.

8) Divestment: The divestment process from a portfolio company usually takes place through: Listing of the financial instruments of that portfolio company on a regulated market; transfer of the investment in this portfolio company to industrial partners (trade sale); transfer of the investment in this portfolio company to other financial investors (secondary buy out); o zeroing of the book value of the investment (write-off).

In short, the private equity fund makes profits when the difference between the consideration received at the time of divestment from a portfolio company is greater than the total capital and other resources made for the investment and enhancement of this portfolio company.

To understand the role of private equity in the business cycle, it is necessary to first examine the latter. The life cycle of a company is conventionally divided into the following phases: (i) Definition of the business idea (seed/development); (ii) start of entrepreneurial activity (start-up); (iii) early growth; (iv) rapid growth; (v) generational change or change of control (replacement/buy-out); and (vi) crisis/restructuring (turnaround)[38].

The need for capital for an entrepreneur basically depends on four variables: Main investments to be made, company profitability, cash flows and turnover growth[39].

By linking the entrepreneurial phases with the four variables mentioned above, it is possible to establish some typical characteristics of each entrepreneurial phase, as summarized in the following table[40].

Table 1 – Schematization of the relationship between the entrepreneurial phase and the main variables that define the capital needs of a company

Entrepreneurial phase	Main investments to be made	Company profitability	Cash Flows	Turnover growth
1. Business idea	Business idea development	Negative	Negative	Data not available

38 GERVASONI A. & SATTIN F. L., *Private equity e venture capital*, op.cit., p.38 ss. DAMIANI E., *Venture Capital e Private Equity*, op.cit., p.19 ss. CASELLI S., *Private Equity and Venture Capital in Europe: Markets, Techniques, and Deals*, op. cit., 8 ss. For further details see: FRIGNANI A., voce *Venture Capital*, in *Noviss. Dig. It.*, App. VII, Turin, Italy, 1987.

39 CASELLI S., *Private Equity and Venture Capital in Europe: Markets, Techniques, and Deals*, op.cit., p. 8 ss.

40 However, it should be noted that the complexity of the business cycle suffers from any schematization and characteristics of two or more business phases can overlap. For further details see: GERVASONI A. & SATTIN F. L., *Private equity e venture capital*, op. cit., p. 38 ss.

2. Start	Supply of production factors	Negative	Negative	First available data
3. Initial growth	Warehouse supply; business development	Negative but improving	Negative but improving	Positive and improving
4. Rapid expansion	Warehouse supply; further business development	Positive and growing	Positive and growing	Positive but worsening
5.Change of control	Warehouse supply; modernization of productive goods	Positive but without growth	Positive but without growth	In decline (towards stagnation)
6.Crisis/ Restructuring	Resolution of crisis state	Descending	Descending	Negative

Source: Elaboration on the basis of the schematization proposed by CASELLI S., *Private Equity and Venture Capital in Europe: Markets, Techniques, and Deals*, op.cit.,p. 9 ss.

To better understand the function of private equity in the entrepreneurial context, it seems useful to relate each entrepreneurial phase with the subjects who could provide capital to serve the typical financial needs of an enterprise in this entrepreneurial phase. The following table will highlight the subjects whose propensity for capital injection, in a specific entrepreneurial phase, is at least medium/high.

Table 2 – Propensity to capital injection in each entrepreneurial phase

	Founders	Strategic partner	Private Equity	Credit institutions	Capital markets
1. Business idea	Middle/ High (strong personal motivation)	Low (difficult to evaluate potential synergies)	Middle/ High (typical activity: start-up intervention)	Low (excessively risky financing)	N/A
2.Start	Average (strong personal motivation but huge	Middle / Low (difficult to evaluate potential synergies)	Middle/ High (typical activity: start-up intervention)	Low (limited period of activity; excessively	N/A

	necessary resources)			risky financing)	
3. Initial growth	Low (huge resources needed)	Average (potential synergies could favor JV)	High (typical activity: development intervention)	Average (except for hostile market conditions or excessive level of indebtedness)	Low (limited period of activity)
4. Rapid expansion	Low (huge resources needed)	Average (potential synergies could favor JV)	High (typical activity: development intervention)	Middle/High (except for hostile market conditions or excessive level of indebtedness)	Middle/ High (except for hostile market conditions)
5. Change of control	Middle/ Low (huge resources needed)	Middle/ High (potential synergies could favor buy-outs or JVs)	High (typical activity: change of control intervention)	Average (except for hostile market conditions or excessive level of indebtedness)	Middle/ High (except for hostile market conditions)
6. Crisis/ Restructuring	Low (huge resources needed)	Low (except clear opportunities to relaunch the activities)	Middle/ High (typical activity: change of control intervention)	Middle/Low (low credit worthiness makes financing too expensive)	N/A

Source: Elaboration on the basis of the schematization proposed by CASELLI S., *Private Equity and Venture Capital in Europe: Markets, Techniques, and Deals*, op.cit., p.11 ss.

From the above scheme, a fundamental characteristic of private equity emerges: Its transversality and versatility of use in each of the entrepreneurial phases, especially in cases where access to traditional channels of business financing (credit institutions and capital markets) is uncertain due to the excessive risk for the potential lender, the strong information asymmetries between the potential lender and the company to be financed, or the limited historical data of the financed company[41].

From a defining point of view, depending on the entrepreneurial phase in which the company being invested is located, a distinction is made between the following types and categories of private equity investments.

Table 3 – Schematization of the main types and categories of investments of private equity by entrepreneurial phase

Entrepreneurial phase	Type	Category
1. Business idea	Start-up intervention	*Venture Capital*
2. Start		
3. Initial growth	Development intervention	*Growth*
4. Rapid expansion		
5. Change of control	Change of control intervention	*Buy-Out*
6.Crisis/Restructuring		

Source: Elaboration on the basis of the schematization proposed by GERVASONI A., SATTIN F. L., *Private equity e venture capital*, cit., 37 ss and CASELLI S., *Private Equity and Venture Capital in Europe: Markets, Techniques, and Deals*, op.cit., p. 9 ss.

In the start-up interventions, typically, the private equity fund acquires a qualified minority stake in the portfolio company, with monitoring and veto rights on the management of this portfolio company. The capital contribution of the fund to the portfolio company is scheduled in stages and, in each phase, subject to the achievement of predetermined results (the literature believes that this technique is particularly effective to

41 CASELLI S., *Private Equity and Venture Capital in Europe: Markets, Techniques, and Deals*, op. cit., p. 9 ss. MHETA V., *Principal-Agent Issues in Private Equity and Venture Capital, in Wharton Research Scholars Journal*, 2004, p. 6. MCCAHERY J. A. & VERMULEN E. P. M., *The Contractual Structure and Regulation of Private Equity Funds and Hedge Funds*, op. cit., 15 ss. COVITZ D. & LIANG N., *Recent Development in the Private Equity Market and the Role of Preferred Returns*, Mimeo, 2002, p.1.

incentivize the management of the portfolio company to achieve results and, to the at the same time, to limit the fund's exposure to the company's risk of failure)[42].

In the interventions for the change of control, the private equity fund acquires a totalitarian or controlling interest in the portfolio company, typically through leveraged buy-outs (therefore with external lenders).

The development interventions, according to the cases, are structured according to the typical features of the interventions for the start or of the interventions for the change of control.

For an idea of the breakdown of the various types of investments in the European private equity market according to the monetary value of these investments, consider that, with reference to the period 2007-2014, the interventions for the start-up represented around 9.1% of investments, development interventions around 9.8% of investments and interventions for change of control represented the remaining 81.1% of investments[43].

For completeness, it is noted that some private equity firms concentrate their activities in a specific industrial sector (for example, the First Reserve Corporation[44] is specialized in the energy sector), in a specific geographical area (for example, the Clessidra SGR[45] is specialized in investments in the Italian market) and/or in a specific entrepreneurial phase (for example, the Apollo Management is specialized in investments for the change of control or recovery of companies in crisis, not also in

---

42 For further information see: SZEGO B., *Finanziarie l'innovazione: il venture capital dopo la riforma del diritto societario*, in *Rivista del diritto commerciale e del diritto generale delle obbligazioni*, vol. I, 2005, p.828 ss. SZEGO B., *Il venture capital come strumento per lo sviluppo delle piccole e medie imprese: un'analisi di adeguatezza dell'ordinamento italiano*, in *Banca d'Italia – Quaderni di ricerca giuridica della Consulenza legale*, n. 55, 2002, p.18 ss.

43 EVCA, 2014 *European Private Equity Activity Data 2007-2014, European Private Equity and Venture Capital Association.* Data extracted from the "Europe Tables-Investments" section of the statistics processed by EVCA and obtained by associating: (i) The "total venture" item with "start-up interventions;" (ii) the item "growth" to "development interventions;" and (iii) the items "buyout," "rescue/turnaround" and "replacement capital" for "interventions for change of control."

44 For institutional information on First Reserve Corporation, see: https://www.firstreserve.com/.

45 For institutional information on Clessidra SGR, see: http://www.clessidrasgr.it/ITA

investments for start-up[46]). It is also possible that the same private equity firm manages multiple funds, each having specific concentrations by industrial sector, geographical area and/or business phase.

A distinction is also made between private equity funds that raise capital exclusively within the corporate group they belong to (called "captive funds"), funds that raise capital exclusively outside the corporate group they belong to (called "independent funds") and finally, funds that raise capital both inside and outside the company group they belong to (called "semi-captive funds").

4. Investment techniques

Private equity investments are normally made using one or more of the investment techniques briefly illustrated below.

1.Company transfer to NewCo: Establishment of a corporate vehicle by, on the one hand, the shareholders of the company subject to the investment (also called "target company") and, on the other hand, the private equity fund; capitalization of the vehicle by contribution of the target company by the shareholders of the target company, and capital injection by the private equity fund. This investment technique is particularly used in start-up interventions[47].

2. Reserved capital increase: Capital increase of the target company reserved for the private equity fund by excluding the right option of the shareholders of the target company. This investment technique is used both in start-up interventions and in interventions for the development.

3. Transfer of company shares: Transfer of company shares from the shareholders of the target company to the private equity fund. This investment technique is particularly used in change of control interventions.

In the context of the interventions for the change of control, a typical technique for purchasing control of a company is leveraged buy-

46 For institutional information on Apollo Management, see: http://www.agm.com/Home.aspx .

47 In practice, the entry of the fund into the capital of the newly created company can take place both during the creation of this new company and after the incorporation through the transfer of company shares by the shareholders of the target company.

out. The term leveraged buy-out (LBO) means a particular investment technique developed in the 1980s in the United States and since then frequently used by private equity funds.

An LBO can be structured in various ways, but in its typical configuration it is made up of three phases: (i) In the first phase, the entity that intends to acquire control of a target company constitutes a corporate vehicle which is subsequently capitalized through capital injections by the party that intends to acquire control and a loan from third parties (for example one or more banks) for the payment of the price of the controlling interest in the aforementioned target company; (ii) in the second phase, the corporate vehicle acquires control of the target company by paying the price of the controlling interest in the target company to the sellers; is (iii) in the third phase, the merger by incorporation of the target company into the corporate vehicle that acquired control is approved. The financing obtained from the acquiring vehicle thus becomes part of the balance sheet of the target company and will be repaid through the future profits of the target company and/or the sale of part of the assets or other assets of the target company[48].

48 For furhter details see: DAMODARAN A., *The Anatomy of an LBO: Leverage, Control and Value*, 2008, http://papers.ssrn.com/sol3/papers.cfm?abstract_id=1162862. MONTALENTI P., *Il leveraged buy-out*, Milan, Italy, Giuffrè, 1991, p.18 ss.

CHAPTER 2
Economic analysis of private equity

1. Economic model of private equity

In this paragraph the economic model of private equity will be reconstructed, starting from the typical organizational structure of a private equity fund and then examining in detail the main economic terms and financial flows in the relationships between private equity fund, limited partners, general partner, advisory company and portfolio companies.

1.1. Organizational structure of the private equity fund

In international practice, private equity funds are organized in the form of a limited partnership or other functionally equivalent legal structure. In the limited partnership, a distinction is made between limited partners, i.e. investors in the private equity fund that provide capital but lack management powers and general partners, i.e. sponsors who have the power to act in the name and on behalf of the fund. For clarity, the limited partners are the investors who confer (or undertake to confer) capital in the fund, while the general partner is the vehicle expression of the sponsors (therefore of the private equity firm) that identifies, analyzes and manages investment opportunities and divestment for the fund[49]. The sponsors provide their consultancy and assistance services to the private equity fund, typically, through a separate corporate vehicle called an "advisory

---

49 For completeness, it is noted that the liability of the limited partners for the obligations of the limited partnership is normally limited to the amount of their contributions unlike the general partner's liability which is unlimited. For further information see: LUBAROFF M. I. & ALTMAN P. M., *Delaware Limited Partnership*, New York, USA, Aspen Publishers, 2013.

company"[50]. A schematic of the typical structure of a private equity fund follows.

For completeness, it is noted that fiscal, regulatory or other specific considerations may require deviations from the typical structure outlined above by inserting a: (i) Parallel fund; (ii) alternative investment vehicle (AIV); (iii) tributary fund; and/or (iv) co-investment vehicle, as briefly illustrated below.

Parallel fund: This invests, divests and carries out any other operation together with the main fund but, typically, it is constituted in a legal system different from the main fund and aims to replicate (as far as possible) the legal architecture of the main fund (it will therefore be managed by the same general partner of the main fund, assisted by the same advisory company of the main fund and subject to the same obligations and charges as the main fund). For example, consider the case where the main fund is established in the United Kingdom but one or more investors (for tax, regulatory or other needs) should, or prefer, invest in a separate fund or a fund established outside the United Kingdom. These investors could merge into a parallel fund which replicates and operates together with the main British fund.

Alternative investment vehicle: This (hereinafter "AIV") invests, divests and carries out any other operation relating to a specific investment together with the main fund (but, unlike the parallel fund, the AIV is created to operate only with reference to a specific investment). For an example, consider the case in which one or more investors (for tax, regulatory or other needs) must, or prefer, participate in a specific investment by means of a vehicle having a structure or residence other than that of the main fund. These investors could merge into an AIV that operates only with reference to this specific investment.

Tributary fund: One or more investors, typically for tax purposes, may prefer to have the capital transferred indirectly through a tributary

---

50 The advisory company typically provides services to multiple private equity funds organized and managed by the same sponsors to achieve economies of scale. Furthermore, in some legal architectures, the same corporate vehicle could play the role of advisory company and general partner. For further information see: NAIDECH S. W., *Private Equity Fund Formation*, New York, USA, Practical Law Company, 2011, p.2.

fund. For example, consider the case in which the direct investment in, or the distribution of proceeds directly from, a main fund determines further tax obligations for investors having a tax residence other than that of the main fund. These investors could flow into a tributary fund which, in turn, would transfer capital into the main fund.

Co-investment vehicle: This invests, divests and carries out any other operation relating to a specific investment pari passu with the main fund but - unlike the AIV, the parallel fund or the main fund - the co-investment vehicle, typically, it is exclusively participated by sponsors and other external investors and does not pay commissions to the general partner or the advisory company. For example, consider, the case in which the sponsors intend to invite new investors to participate in an investment opportunity that the main fund alone would not be able to achieve.

1.2. Economic terms and financial flows

The economic terms of the relationships between private equity funds, limited partners, general partners, advisory companies and portfolio companies vary from case to case, are influenced by the experience of the sponsors, by the conditions of the international financial markets and are the result of negotiations between the parties. However, there are some basic economic terms, briefly illustrated below, which apply to each private equity fund.

Capital injections: Investors undertake to provide capital to the fund within the times and within the maximum amount agreed in the investment contract in the private equity fund. In particular, investors undertake to provide capital when requested by the general partner so that the financial funding necessary to meet the fund's management costs and, above all, the fund's investments in portfolio companies[51] is formed. The fund's assets under management indicate the total amount of capital that the fund may request to be transferred by its investors. Generally, investors cannot increase their share of capital injections into the fund or request

51 MCCAHERY J. A. & VERMEULEN E. P. M., *The Contractual Structure and Regulation of Private Equity Funds and Hedge Funds*, in *LSE Working Paper*, n. 50/2008, 2008, p., 9 ss.

liquidation before maturity (typically within ten to thirteen years of setting up the fund)[52].

Management fees: The fund pays management fees annually to the advisory company (therefore indirectly to the private equity firm), ranging between 1.5% and 2.5% - typically 2% - of the assets managed by the fund (i.e. total capital that the fund may request to be transferred to its investors)[53]. The management fees are normally payable on a quarterly or half-yearly basis and regardless of the amount of investments made by the fund or their fate. For example, in the case of a fund with € 500 million of assets under management and annual management fees equal to 2% of the assets under management, the fees in question would be € 10 million for each year of the fund's life, even if the fund only used part of its assets for investments in portfolio companies and also in the event that all investments had negative returns.

Performance fees: At the time of distribution of the proceeds from the investment and divestment activities of the fund, the general partner (expression of the sponsors) receives a percentage, typically 20%, of any profits of the fund by way of performance fees[54].

Direct investment: It is a practice that the private equity firm, through the general partner, invests in the fund alongside the limited partners. The measure of direct investment varies according to the size of the fund but is typically between 1% and 5% of the assets managed by the fund (the percentage is inversely proportional to the amount of assets managed)[55].

---

52 COVITZ D. & LIANG N., *Recent Development in the Private Equity Market and the Role of Preferred Returns*, Mimeo, 2002, p. 7. PHALIPPOU L., *Beware of Venturing into Private Equity*, in *Journal of Economic Perspectives*, vol. 23, n. 1, 2009, p.150.

53 PREQIN, *2013 Preqin Investor Network Global Alternatives Report Fund Terms and Conditions*, New York, USA, Preqin Investor Network, 2013, p.91. DE MARIA C., *Introduction to private equity*, cit., 54. NAIDECH S. W., *Private Equity Fund Formation*, op.cit., p.8. COVITZ D. & LIANG N., *Recent Development in the Private Equity Market and the Role of Preferred Returns*, op.cit., p.7.

54 PREQIN, *2013 Preqin Investor Network Global Alternatives Report Fund Terms and Conditions*, op.cit., p.94. COVITZ D. & LIANG N., *Recent Development in the Private Equity Market and the Role of Preferred Returns*, op.cit., p.7.

55 PREQIN, 2013 *Preqin Investor Network Global Alternatives Report Fund Terms and Conditions*, op.cit., p.93. DE MARIA C., *Introduction to private equity*, op. cit., p.54. NAIDECH S. W., *Private Equity Fund Formation*, op.cit., p.8.

Services rendered to portfolio companies: The latters pay the advisory company (therefore, indirectly, to the private equity firm) commissions or fees for services rendered by the advisory company to portfolio companies (for example, for services rendered by professionals of the advisory company as directors of portfolio companies or as consultants to portfolio companies for extraordinary corporate transactions or simply for the monitoring of portfolio companies).

Services rendered to the fund and other fees: Fees, expenses and costs for services rendered to the fund by third parties (e.g. the fund's initial organization fees[56] and other legal fund or financial advisors fees) are directly charged to the fund and are therefore borne by the investors. The advisory company may also charge flat-rate fees to the fund following the realization of an investment or a corporate transaction (transaction fees).

Proceeds distribution: The proceeds from the management of the fund are typically distributed to investors, making sure that the limited partners receive, primarily, the repayment of their capital injections. In some cases, the fund regulations provide that performance fees are paid to the general partner only after a priority distribution of the fund's proceeds in favor of limited partners such as to ensure them a minimum return (hurdle rate), typically equal to an internal rate yield of 5%-9% of the capital contributed[57]. Finally, a distinction is made between distributions according to the "american" and "european" method (in which the performance fees are calculated and liquidated at the end of each investment cycle in a portfolio company) and distributions according to the "european method" (in which the commissions on the performances are calculated and liquidated only at the end of the fund and therefore at the end of the last investment cycle)[58].

---

56 Usually the costs and expenses for the organization of the fund are flat-rate quantified in an amount equal to 1% of the assets managed by the fund. See: DE MARIA C., *Introduction to private equity*, op.cit., p.54.

57 PREQIN, *2013 Preqin Investor Network Global Alternatives Report Fund Terms and Conditions*, op.cit., p.92. DE MARIA C., *Introduction to private equity*, op.cit., p.56.

58 NAIDECH S. W., *Private Equity Fund Formation*, op.cit., p.6 ss.

To illustrate the above, assume a private equity fund that has the following characteristics: (i) Assets under management, € 500 million; (ii) annual management fees, 2% of the assets under management; (iii) performance fees, 20% of profits with 7% internal hurdle rate; (iv) direct investment by the general partner, 1% of assets under management; (v) term of the fund, 10 years ; (vi) proceeds from the closure of the fund € 1,200 million. For simplicity, it is also assumed that there are no expenses, charges or commissions charged to the fund, that all investments are made when the fund is established and that all divestments are made at the end of the fund. The distribution of proceeds, at the end of the tenth year since the establishment of the fund, will take place as follows:

a) to investors, pro quota among themselves, € 500 million as a refund of capital injections;

b) to investors, pro quota among them, approximately € 483 million as a priority distribution relating to the internal guaranteed rate of return (hurdle rate) of 7% [59];

c) to the general partner, € 140 million in performance fees[60];

d) to investors, pro-rata among themselves, the remaining € 77 million by way of profit distribution[61].

In the ten-year period, gross revenues for the private equity firm amounted to approximately € 240 million (of which € 100 million as management fees in favor of the advisory company, therefore fixed remuneration, and approximately € 140 million to performance fees, therefore variable remuneration) as well as a return of approximately € 11 million against a direct investment of € 5 million.

2. Remuneration of the private equity firm

In this paragraph the main economic terms relating to the remuneration of the private equity firm will be analyzed. The economic analysis that follows is aimed at highlighting the critical issues of

---

59 The calculation is made explicit: [(1.07 ^ 10) * € 500 million] - € 500 million = approximately € 983 million - € 500 million = approximately € 483 million.

60 The calculation is made explicit: 0.2 * (€ 1,200 million - € 500 million) = 0.2 * € 700 million = € 140 million.

61 The calculation is made explicit: € 1,200 million - € 500 million - approximately € 483 million - € 140 million = approximately € 77 million.

remuneration policies according to current market terms. Finally, recommendations relating to the remuneration of the private equity firm will be proposed for a better alignment of the interests of the parties.

2.1. Remuneration, incentives and risks of opportunistic behavior of the private equity firm

The remuneration of the private equity firm is a topic of growing interest, especially after part of the financial press and economic doctrine have criticized the remuneration policies of private equity firms considering them excessively burdensome and unbalanced in favor of private equity firms[62]. Specifically, the private equity firm is indirectly remunerated through four channels: (i) Management fees in favor of the advisory company; (ii) performance fees in favor of the general partner; (iii) proceeds from the direct investment in favor of the general partner; and (iv) consideration for services rendered to portfolio companies and other commissions in favor of the advisory company. Each of the four remuneration channels will be analyzed below in order to determine in which cases, and to what extent, the interests of the private equity firm and investors diverge.

Management fees: The annual management fees, payable by the private equity fund to the advisory company, are typically equal to 2% of the assets managed by the fund. Since the fund normally has a duration of ten years, in absolute terms, it must generate profits of at least 25%[63] of the assets under management only to offset the cost of the fees in question. The economic weight of the management fees falls (substantially) on the investors and (indirectly) benefits the private equity firm. The private

62 PHALIPPOU L., *Beware of Venturing into Private Equity, in Journal of Economic Perspectives*, op.cit., p.150. MCCRUM D., *Private Equity Profits called into questions*, in *Financial Times*, 23 January 2012.

63 Assume a fund whose assets under management is € 500 million, which has a duration of 10 years and whose annual management fees are equal to 2% of the assets under management. In this case the total paid by the fund in management fees over the 10 years will be € 100 million and the capital available for investments will be € 400 million. To offset the cost of management fees, the fund will have to generate a return of at least 25% of the capital available for investment (€400m*X=€100m; X=€100m/€400m; X=25%). IANNOTTA, G., *Investment Banking – A Guide to Underwriting and Advisory Services*, Berlin, Germany, Springer-Verlag, 2010, p.19 ss.

equity firm has incentives to create funds whose assets under management is ever greater and to minimize the operating costs of the advisory company, because the management fees are directly proportional to the assets under management to the fund and are not related to the performance of the fund. nor to the operating costs incurred by the advisory company[64]. It is also noted that the incentives of the private equity firm could lead to the formation of an oversized fund with respect to the offer of investments in portfolio companies, such as to prevent the fund from using all the assets under management or from inducing the fund to carry out sub-optimal investments. As critically observed by some authors, it has happened that the amount of the commissions in question became significant to the point of constituting about 2/3 of the revenues expected by some private equity firms regardless of the performance of their private equity funds[65]. In short, the management fees, as typically structured (i.e. 2% of the assets under management for each year of activity of the fund), generate a misalignment of the interests of the parties because they remunerate the private equity firm even in the event that the returns of the fund are negative or lower than expected. From a qualitative point of view, the interests of the parties are always misaligned, however the misalignment is less pronounced if the return of the fund is positive because, in this case, the utility (for investors) deriving from the higher return of the fund would compensate for the disutility (for investors) resulting from the cost of management fees[66].

Performance fees: They are payable by the fund to the general partner; are typically equal to 20% of any profits of the fund and are payable only after a priority distribution of any profits in favor of the limited partners in order to ensure them a minimum return on capital conferred. Performance fees have characteristics similar to a fund option

64 BAKS K. P. & BENVENISTE L. M., *Alignment of Interest in the Private Equity Industry*, in *Emory Center for Alternative Investments papers*, 2010, p. 6ss. GILLIGAN J. & WRIGHT M., *Private Equity Demistified: An Explanatory Guide*, op. cit., p.2.

65 METRICK A. & YASUDA A., *The Economics of Private Equity Funds*, in *Review of Financial Studies*, vol. 23, 2010, pp.2303-2341.

66 GILLIGAN J. & WRIGHT M., *Private Equity Demistified: An Explanatory Guide*, op.cit., p.2.

purchase option[67]: Just as a purchase option would be exercised only if it generates profits, so performance fees are due only in the case of fund profits. Their value is therefore a function: (i) of the expected return on investments made by the fund[68];(ii) the volatility of the investment returns made by the fund[69]; (iii) of the time remaining until the fund expires; (iv) of the capital contributed by investors and of the possible internal minimum rate of return (hurdle rate) of the fund; and (v) the timing and priorities in the distribution of the fund's proceeds. Only the expected return on investments and their volatility - therefore the points (i) and (ii) above - depend on the investment choices of the general partner and will therefore be isolated and analyzed[70]. As for the expected return, the interests of the general partner and investors are perfectly aligned because, other factors being equal, between two possible investments, the general partner will have an incentive to choose the investment with the highest expected return. As for volatility, the value of performance fees (such as a buy option) increases as the volatility (therefore of the risk profile) of the fund's investment portfolio increases, which means that the general partner's risk appetite it is not aligned with that of the investors because the general partner participates in the eventual profits of these investments to an extent more than proportional to its direct investment. It is therefore necessary to examine the correlation between the expected return of the

67 FENN G. W., LIANG N. & PROWSE S., *The Private Equity Market: An Overview*, in *Financial Markets, Institutions, and Instruments*, vol. 6, n. 4., 1997, pp.1-106. SAHLMAN W. A., *The Structure and Governance of Venture Capital Organization*, in *Journal of Financial Economics*, vol. 27, 1990, pp.473-521.

68 By expected return on an investment, we mean the weighted average of the possible future returns of that investment, where the weighting factors are represented by the respective probabilities of realization (for example, if an investment of € 100 is expected to have a return of € 120 with a 60% probability and a yield of € 90 with a 40% probability, the expected return will be € 120 * 0.6 + € 90 * 0.4 = € 72 + € 36 = € 108). For further information see: BREALEY R. A., MYERS S. C. & ALLEN F., *Principles of Corporate Finance. Global Edition*, New York, USA, McGraw-Hill/Irwin, 2011, pp.193 ss.

69 By volatility of the returns on investments made by the fund, we mean the measure of the likely change in these returns; volatility measures the amplitude of the swing (not the sense). For further information see: BREALEY R. A., MYERS S. C. & ALLEN F., *Principles of Corporate Finance. Global Edition.*, op.cit., p.80 ss.

70 BAKS K. P. & BENVENISTE L. M., *Alignment of Interest in the Private Equity Industry*, 2010, available at: http://goizueta.emory.edu/Faculty/cai/documents/ECAI_Alignment.pdf,, p.6 ss.

fund and the incentives of the general partner to increase the volatility (therefore of the risk profile) of the investment portfolio of the fund. The general partner will have incentives to increase the volatility (therefore the risk profile) of the investment portfolio for maximize the probability, albeit remote, of receiving payment of the performance fees, when the expected return of the fund is negative (i.e. such that the fund is not even able to repay the capital contributed by the investors). The general partner will have even stronger incentives to increase the volatility (therefore the risk profile) of the fund's investment portfolio, so as to increase the expected value of its performance fees, when, on the other hand, the expected return of the fund is neutral (i.e. such as to expect that the fund will be able to repay the capital contributed by the investors together with the priority distribution reserved for them and that the performance fees may be payable). This explains why in the scenario in question the probability of receiving commissions on performance is greater. Finally, when the return of the fund is positive (i.e. such as to expect profits to be distributed to investors and that performance fees are payable), the general partner will have incentives to increase the volatility (therefore the risk profile) of the investment portfolio, although lower than the scenario in which the expected return of the fund is neutral. This explains why in the scenario in question the general partner will have an interest in not increasing the risk to the point of compromising the payment of the performance fees completely.

Proceeds from direct investment: The direct investment of the general partner (therefore, indirectly, of the private equity firm) in the fund is typically between 1% and 5% of the assets managed by the fund. This direct investment is obviously aimed at aligning the interests of the general partner and the limited partners, taking place under the same conditions[71]. However, in practice, direct investment can also take place by clearing or waiving future credits (for example credits related to management fees). Although the source of financing of the direct investment of the general partner may seem irrelevant, behavioral finance seems to suggest that the incentives of the general partner would be more aligned with those of the

71 DE MARIA C., *Introduction to private equity*, op.cit., p.55.

limited partners if the investment is made using capital own of the general partner or indebtedness (thus sacrificing part of the existing assets)[72].

Assuming that the general partner's direct investment takes place with equity, this investment should align the interests of the parties in all the fund's return scenarios.

Fee for services rendered to portfolio companies and other commissions. The private equity firm has strong incentives to offer services and carry out activities that generate commissions in favor of the general partner, the advisory company or other subjects affiliated or attributable to the private equity firm. These incentives are in conflict with investors' interest in minimizing the cost of the services offered to the fund or portfolio companies (the economic weight of which is essentially borne by investors). In some cases, the advisory company charges the transaction fees fund for corporate transactions relating to portfolio companies (for example, investments, divestments, capital increases and other extraordinary corporate transactions). The charge of these fees, being disconnected from the fees or costs for the advisory company, seems to create incentives for the advisory company to carry out corporate transactions or pursue other opportunities that may generate commissions.

Overall, the remuneration of the private equity firm according to current market terms creates a misalignment between the interests of the private equity firm and those of the investors which is more marked in the scenario in which the expected return of the fund is neutral, lower in the scenario in which the expected return of the fund is negative and minimum in the scenario where the expected return of the fund is positive. Below is

---

72 This seems at least partly attributable to the so-called "endowment effect," a notion introduced by Thaler, see: THALER R. H., *Toward a Positive Theory of Consumer Choice*, in *Journal of Economic Behavior and Organization,* vol. 1, 2008, pp.39-60. In particular, the endowment effect was illustrated through a series of experiments (conducted by Kahneman, Knetsch and Thaler) in which a group of individuals are given a cup of breakfast and allowed to sell it or exchange it for another good; research shows that the price at which individuals are willing to sell the cup is about twice the price at which the same individuals would be willing to buy it. The endowment effect therefore lies in the divergence between "willingness to accept" and "willingness to pay" and, specifically, concerns the tendency to attribute greater value to an asset when it is in possession, for further information see: KAHNEMAN, D., KNETSCH, J. L., & THALER, R. H., *Experimental Tests of the Endowment Effect and the Coase Theorem*, in *Journal of Political Economy*, vol. 98, no. 6, 1990, p.1325 ss.

a table that summarizes the results of the above qualitative investigation relating to the alignment/misalignment of the interests of the private equity firm and of investors in a private equity fund, according to the expected return of this fund.

Table 4 –Schematic alignment/misalignment of private equity firm (vs) investor interests based on the expected return of the fund

	Expected return of the private equity fund	
	Negative(*)	**Neutral(**)**
Management fees	Unaligned	Unaligned
Commissions on performance	Mild misalignment/ negligible	Unaligned
Direct investment	Aligned	Aligned
Fees for services and other commissions	Unaligned	Unaligned

(*)no profits; no capital repayment to investors.

(**)

capital repayment to investors; limited profits; possible payment of performance fees

(***)

capital repayment to investors; profits that generate performance fees

Source: Elaboration based on: BAKS K. P. & BENVENISTE L.M., *Alignment of Interest in the Private Equity Industry*, op.cit., p.6 ss.

2.2. Recommendations for better alignment of the interests of the private equity firm and investors

Having observed that the remuneration of the private equity firm according to current market terms creates a misalignment between the interests of the private equity firm and the interests of investors, it remains to be determined whether and which corrective measures can be introduced. In this perspective, various options will be illustrated below according to which to structure the four main channels of this remuneration - that is, management fees, performance fees, proceeds from direct investment and fees for services rendered to portfolio companies or other fees - in order to determine which options make it possible to align the interests of the parties more closely.

Management fees: The current market terms relating to management fees provide for the annual payment of a percentage (1.5% - 2.5%) of the assets managed by the fund. This creates a mismatch between the interests of the private equity fund and the investors because the fees are not related to the fund's return and they remunerate the private equity firm exclusively in low to the size of the fund. Also in light of market practice, management fees may appear to be structured according to at least four options which will be briefly illustrated and analyzed below:

1.Fixed percentage (1.5% -2.5%) of the sum of: (i) Market value of the investments made and (ii) capital available to the fund. This option was frequently used in the U.S. market in the 1980s but subsequently abandoned, probably because it was too expensive and complex to manage[73]. The correlation between the amount of the commissions and the market value of the investments seems to be able to align (even if only partially) the incentives of the parties to maximize the returns of the fund. However, the option in question appears problematic because: (i) It creates conflicts between the parties - or at least additional costs - for the determination of the market value of the investments; and (ii) could incentivize the private equity fund to delay divestments even when the interests of investors would be maximized by faster divestments, since they would be reduced by management fees for the advisory company. Compared to current market terms, option (1) seems to worsen both for the private equity firm and for investors.

2. In the first 5 years, fixed percentage (1.5% -2.5%) of assets under management; subsequently, a progressive reduction of this percentage. This option recognizes that after the end of the investment cycle (typically after the fifth year since the formation of the fund) the advisory company's charges are lower and, therefore, the management fees must be adequate. Compared to current market terms, option (2)

73 IANNOTTA, G., *Investment Banking – A Guide to Underwriting and Advisory Services*, Berlin, Germany, Springer-Verlag, 2010, p.22 ss.

appears to be better for investors because it reduces the overall amount of the fees in question, however the management fees are not related to the return of the fund and, therefore, the interests of the parties are not they seem perfectly aligned.

3.Total or partial compensation between management and monitoring fees for portfolio companies. Some private equity firms have recently announced their intention to review the calculation mechanisms of some commissions, anticipating the possibility that the management fees may be compensated (in whole or in part) with the monitoring fees charged to the portfolio companies[74]. This option (suggested by the private equity firms themselves) seems to postulate (and therefore admit) that the current market terms generate a duplication of remuneration for the private equity firm. Compared to current market terms, option (3) appears to be an improvement for investors, however the management fees are not related to the return of the fund and, therefore, the interests of the parties are not perfectly aligned.

4. Management commissions equal to operating costs of the advisory company. This option intends to eliminate the remuneration value of the management fees, leaving them the task of reimbursing the advisory company for the costs incurred by it for the operational management of the fund. Option (4) appears to be higher than current market terms and other options because, by depriving the commissions of a remunerative value, it eliminates the main distorting factor of the alignment between the interests of investors and the interests of the private equity firm.

Performance fees: The current market terms relating to performance fees provide for the payment of fees equal to 20% of any profits of the fund, after a priority distribution of any profits in favor of the limited partners so that they receive a minimum return on the capital conferred (hurdle rate) equal to an internal rate of return of 5% -9%. This can create a mismatch between the interests of the private equity fund and investors. Also in light of market practice, management fees may appear

---

74 MAREMONT M. & SPECTOR M., *Blackstone to Curb Controversial Fee Practice*, in *Wall Street Journal*, 7 October 2014, http://online.wsj.com/articles/blackstone-to-curb-controversial-fee-practice-1412714245.

to be structured according to, at least, three options which will be briefly illustrated and analyzed below:

1.Payment of performance fees according to the "American" model (i.e. at the end of each investment cycle)[75]. In this option, the proceeds from the divestment are distributed at the end of each investment cycle (not when the fund is closed). This option seems, however, to exacerbate the misalignment of the parties' interests because it would allow the private equity firm to collect performance fees even if the overall return of the fund is negative (for example if the fund has generated only one positive investment whose profits are lower than the losses generated by all other investments). Specifically, this option would encourage the taking of excessive risks and the delay of divestments whose expected return is negative or does not seem to entail payments of performance fees.

2.Payment of performance fees according to the "American" model with compensation mechanism between investments and adjustment of the amount of performance fees. Like option (1) but with a malus or return mechanism (claw back) in the event that, in consideration of the overall return of the fund, excess fees have been paid. This option seems superior to option (1), because the performance fees would be parameterised to the overall performance of the fund. However, additional costs would be created for the monitoring and implementation of the compensation and adjustment mechanisms[76].

3.Payment of performance fees according to the "European" model (i.e. at the end of the fund's life cycle). This option seems superior to the previous ones because it causes the performance fees to be parameterised to the overall return of the fund but does not provide for additional costs and charges.

However, in none of the above options it seems possible to completely eliminate the risk that the private equity firm takes excessive

---

75 SCHELL J., *Private Equity Funds. Business Structure and Operations*, New York, USA, Law Journal Press, 2006.

76 For the sake of completeness, it should be noted that, in the event that the adjustment mechanism provides for the simple repayment of the excess payment received without interest, the private equity firm could have an incentive - out of alignment with the interests of the investors - to delay divestments with negative expected return for the purpose. to postpone repayment of overpayments and continue to benefit from the return on those overpayments.

risks (so as to increase the volatility of the investment portfolio and, therefore, increase the expected value of the performance fees) by simply changing the economic terms and the payment time for performance fees.

Proceeds from direct investment. The current market terms relating to the direct investment of the general partner (therefore, indirectly, of the private equity firm) in the fund provide for an investment of between 1% and 5% of the assets managed by the fund, based on the size of the fund. As illustrated, this investment generally aligns the incentives of the parties. However, the economic literature emphasizes the greater effectiveness of a direct investment made by means of disbursement of capital compared to one made by renunciation of future credits. It is also noted that the greater the disutility for the private equity firm resulting from the loss of direct investment, the greater the alignment of interests between private equity firm and investors. With this in mind, it would be desirable that the general partner's direct investment is non-transferable until the expiry of the fund to ensure the continuation of the alignment of interests.

Fee for services rendered to portfolio companies and other commissions. The current market terms provide for the charging of costs for services rendered by the advisory company to the portfolio companies. In some cases, the advisory company may also charge transaction fees for corporate transactions. The conflict of interest between private equity firm and investors arises from the fact that the private equity firm may have incentives to offer services and carry out activities that generate commissions in favor of the general partner, the advisory company or other affiliated or attributable subjects to the private equity firm. It does not seem possible to eliminate the risk of opportunistic behavior of the private equity firm with reference to the offer of services to portfolio companies by modifying only the economic terms of the fees. However, corporate transaction fees should be eliminated as they are unrelated to the fund's return and potentially duplicate the remuneration of the private equity firm.

Overall, the main recommendations for improving the alignment of the interests of the private equity firm and of investors with reference to the economic terms of the remuneration of the private equity firm can be summarized as follows:

Table 5 – Recommendations to improve the alignment between private equity firm interests and investor interests

	Risks deriving from remuneration according to current market terms	Reccomandations
Management fees	Not related to fund performance; they create an incentive to increase the size of the fund with the consequent risk that the fund may not use all the assets under management or use it in sub-optimal investments.	Management fees related to operating costs for the private equity firm (not to the assets under management).
Performance fees	Private equity firm participates, more than proportionally to its direct investment, in the profits but not in the losses of the fund (economic model similar to the purchase option); private equity firm has an incentive to increase the volatility of the investment portfolio to maximize the expected value of performance fees.	Distribution of any profits to the private equity firm according to the "European method" (i.e. closing the fund and not closing each individual investment cycle in portfolio companies).
Direct investment	If direct investment is not made through the outlay of own capital, there is a risk that the private equity firm will not feel that it has "interests at stake" and take excessive risks in managing the investment portfolio.	Direct investment made through the outlay of own capital; prohibition to transfer the participation of the general partner in the fund.
Fees for services and other commissions	Private equity firm has an incentive to maximize services offered to portfolio companies as a source of revenues and, if transaction fees are envisaged, to involve portfolio companies in corporate operations that generate the payment of these commissions for corporate operations.	Private equity firm has an incentive to maximize services offered to portfolio companies as a source of revenues and, if transaction fees are envisaged, to involve portfolio companies in corporate operations

		that generate the payment of these commissions for corporate operations.

Source: Elaboration based on BAKS K. P. & BENVENISTE L.M., *Alignment of Interest in the Private Equity Industry*, op.cit., p.6 ss.

The above recommendations are in line with the guidelines and best practices proposed by the International Limited Partners Association (ILPA)[77], but above all with the obligations on remunerative policies and practices set out in the European Directive 2011/61/EU on managers alternative investment funds (hereinafter, the "AIFM Directive") as well as with the guidelines of the European Securities and Markets Authority (ESMA) for sound remuneration policies pursuant to the AIFM Directive[78].

For the sake of completeness, it should be noted that the qualitative analysis of the misalignment between the interests of the private equity firm and the interests of investors created by the current market terms relating to the (indirect) remuneration of the private equity firm and the illustration of possible options aimed at mitigating this misalignment does not take into consideration the reputational cost that a

---

77 ILPA, *Private Equity Principles*, v. 2.0, 2011, p. 5, http://ilpa.org/ilpa-private-equity-principles/, according to which: "Management fees should be based on reasonable operating expenses and reasonable salaries, as excessive fees create misalignment of interests" and "[a]lignment of interest between [limited partners] and [general partners] is best achieved when [general partners]' wealth creation is primarily derived from carried interest and returns generated from a substantial equity commitment to the fund, and when [general partners] receive a percentage of profits after [limited partners] return requirements are met. [General partner] wealth creation from excessive management, transaction or other fees and proceeds sources, reduces alignment of interest. We continue to believe that a [general partner]'s own capital at risk serves as the greatest incentive for alignment of interests. [General partner] equity interests in funds primarily made through cash contributions result in higher alignment of interest with [limited partners] compared to those made through the waiver of management fees."

78 See, in particular, art. 13 of Directive 2011/61/EU according to which Member States impose on fund managers the obligation to apply "remunerative policies and practices that reflect and promote sound and effective risk management and that do not encourage risk-taking inconsistent with the risk profiles, with the regulations or the constituent documents of the [alternative investment funds] they manage ." See also Annex II of Directive 2011/61/EU and the ESMA/2013/232 guidelines of 1 July 2013 entitled "Guidelines for sound remuneration policies pursuant to the AIFM Directive."

private equity firm would face in taking opportunistic behavior to the detriment of its investors[79]. In particular, in the event that the private equity firm implements opportunistic conduct, the risk would be that it encounters greater difficulties in the raising of capital by investors for the creation and organization of new funds.

Finally, it should be noted that a recent survey conducted among investors in private equity funds shows the growing perception (by investors) that the current market terms relating to the remuneration of the private equity firm - the so-called "two and twenty"[80] - are unable to align the interests of the parties and that it is necessary to review, with priority, the current economic terms relating to management and performance fees. It has also been observed that investor pressure to reduce management fees has recently resulted in the growing use of co-investment structures - usually reserved for extraordinary interventions by investors outside the fund- thanks to which investors can participate in the investment opportunity pari passu with the fund and without paying management fees or performance fees[81]. It is evident that the generalized use of co-investment structures would annihilate the economic model of private

---

79 For an analysis of the deterrent effect of reputational costs limited to the venture capital market see: ATANASOV V., IVANOV V. & LITVAK K., *Does Reputation Limit Opportunistic Behavior in The VC Industry? Evidence from Litigation against VCs*, in *Journal of Finance*, vol. 67, n. 6, 2012, p.2215 ss. After examining a sample of litigation relating to venture capital firms, the authors conclude that more established venture capital firms are less likely to be sued and that the reputational costs for a venture capital firm act as a deterrent against opportunistic behavior. It should be noted, however, that the research was conducted with reference to a limited subjective area and cannot be generalized to the private equity market in the absence of further research and empirical evidence.

80 In practice, the "two and twenty" model -with particular reference to the funds specializing in interventions for change of control- means the complex of the following market terms for the remuneration of the private equity firm: (i) Commissions management of 2% of the assets managed by the fund; (ii) performance fees 20% of profits; (iii) minimum guaranteed internal rate (hurdle rate) 5% -9%; and (iv) direct investment of the general partner in the capital of the fund 1% -5% of the assets under management. PREQIN, *2013 Preqin Investor Network Global Alternatives Report Fund Terms and Conditions*, op.cit., p. 94 ss.

81 PREQIN, 2013 *Preqin Investor Network Global Alternatives Report Fund Terms and Conditions*, op. cit., p.40 ss. MCCAHERY J. A. & VERMEULEN E. P. M., *Recasting Private Equity Funds after the Financial Crisis: The End of 'Two and Twenty' and the Emergence of Co-Investment and Separate Account Arrangements*, in *ECGI – Law Working Paper*, n. 231/2013, 2013.

equity which postulates the payment of management and performance fees and it is equally evident that market surveys confirm the pressure of investors to revise the model of the "two and twenty" in the search for a system that allows greater alignment between the interests of private equity firms and the interests of investors. The foregoing reinforces the considerations and recommendations made for better alignment of the interests of the parties.

3. Economic impact of private equity: Value creation

This section will critically reconstruct the complex framework relating to the economic impact of private equity. The reconstruction will start from the criticisms made by the public opinion, to then analyze the studies of the economic literature and will end with the illustration of an innovative thesis that connects private equity with the debt capital market (i.e. business financing).

3.1. Public opinion and private equity

Franz Münterfering (a member of the German social-democratic party) compared private equity firms to "swarms of locusts that land on businesses, plundering them before going further"[82]. in 2005. In the following years, especially following the "sub-prime" mortgage crisis, public opinion has continued to investigate the economic impact of private equity with growing suspicion and the extravagances of some members of the European Parliament have certainly not gone unnoticed and without criticism while the real economy suffered one of the worst economic crises since the great depression of 1929[83].Opponents of Mitt Romney, partner of the private equity fund Bain Capital and candidate for the US presidency in 2012, further fueled the debate arguing that the goal of

---

82 THE ECONOMIST, *Locust, pocus*, in *The Economist*, 5 May 2005, http://www.economist.com/node/3935994, in which the words of Franz Münterfering: "Swarms of locusts that fall on companies, stripping them bare before moving on."

83 This refers in particular to the millionaire engagement paid for the private performance, lasting about 30 minutes, of singer Rod Stewart on the occasion of the birthday party of the Chairman and CEO of the Blackstone Group fund in 2008.STEWART J. B., *The Birthday Party. How Stephen Schwarzman became private equity's designated villain*, in The New Yorker, 11 February 2008, http://www.newyorker.com/magazine/2008/02/11/the-birthday-party-2.

private equity firms "is not to create jobs (...) but to create wealth for themselves and their investors"[84]. There was no lack of more moderate interventions, in which it was recognized that the economic literature does not fully support the positions of the detractors of private equity[85]. The fact remains that public opinion still sees private equity with suspicion, probably due to the confidentiality or opacity, depending on the point of view, with which the industry was able to operate before the recent regulatory reforms[86].

3.1.1. Analysis of the doctrine

Also in order to be able to analytically evaluate the criticisms made by public opinion to private equity, the conclusions reached by the doctrine on the economic impact of private equity will be analyzed below, with particular regard to the following issues: (i) If and to what extent private equity generates profits for private equity firms and for investors in private equity funds; (ii) what are the effects of private equity on portfolio companies and stakeholders (including, for example, workers, social creditors and commercial suppliers); and (iii) if the net economic effect of private equity is positive and it therefore creates value.

3.1.2. Negative remarks: (i) Mere financial artifice; (ii) excessive indebtedness; (iii) reduction in employment levels; (iv) profits payable by taxpayers; and (v) modest returns

Private equity detractors argue that private equity does not create value but, at the most, transfers wealth from less experienced or organized entities (for example, small shareholders, creditors, workers or taxpayers) to private equity firms and, sometimes, even to those which invest in

84 BRITTAIN B., *Obama compares Romney's rhetoric to 'cow pie of distortion'*, in *CNN Politics*, 25 May 2012, http://whitehouse.blogs.cnn.com/2012/05/25/obama-compares-romneys-rhetoric-to-cow-pie-of-distortion/,in which the words of Barack Obama are reported:" [T]he main goal of a financial firm like Gov. Romney's is not to create jobs. Their main goal is to create wealth for themselves and their investors."
85 DAVIDOFF S. M., *Dealbook; With Private Equity Under Attack, Academia Tries to Quantify Its Value*, in *The New York Times*, 25 January 2012.
86 SPANGLER T., *Private Equity's Public Image Issues*, in *Forbes*, 4 October 2013.

private equity funds organized by these private equity firms[87]. In this perspective, private equity would be an ingenious technique by which private equity firms take ownership of profits and outsource losses[88]. Taking the expression from the game theory, private equity would be a zero-sum game (i.e. a game in which the gain or loss of one subject is perfectly balanced by the corresponding loss or gain of another subject)[89]. The main arguments put forward by private equity detractors will be analyzed in greater detail below.

Mere financial device: Michael Gordon (at the time responsible for the investments of Fidelity International, one of the largest financial groups and pension funds) defined private equity "nothing more than a financial engineering artifice, however awkward"[90] in 2008. The reference is evidently to acquisitions by means of leveraged buy-outs, without operational improvements for the portfolio companies and which result in mere financial transactions. To illustrate the point, assume a mature company, without financial debt, with the ability to generate stable cash flows and whose business value (in the absence of equity and financial debt) is € 100 million. It is also assumed that a private fund purchases 100% of the capital of the company in question through leveraged buy-outs with a debt: Equity ratio of 7: 3, that is, with a financial funding consisting of € 70 million of debt provided by third parties and € 30 million of own risk capital. Finally, it is assumed that over time the company in question does not achieve improvements or suffer worsening in conducting its business and that there are no extraordinary events such as

---

87 DE FONTENAY E., *Private Equity Firms As Gatekeepers*, in *Review of Banking & Financial Law*, vol. 33, 2013, p.125.

88 LUZZATTO GARDNER A., *Romney's Bain Yielded Private Gains, Socialized Losses*, in *Bloomberg*, 16 July 2012, http://www.bloomberg.com/news/2012-07-15/romney-s-bain-yielded- private-gains-socialized-losses.html.

89 For further details see: COOTER R., MATTEI U., MONATERI P. G., PARDOLESI R. & ULEN T., *Il mercato delle regole – Analisi economica del diritto civile*, Bologna, Italy, Il Mulino, 2006, p.54 ss. FUDENBERG D. & TIROLE J., *Game Theory*, Cambridge, US, The MIT Press, 1991.

90 GORDON M., *Private equity boom was nothing more than a clumsy trick*, in *Financial Times*, 31 March 2008, http://www.ft.com/cms/s/0/9a495d2a-ff34-11dc-b556-000077b07658.html, according to which: "[T]he boom in private equity, which was promoted as the superior business model, based on patient capital, superior management and an alignment of interests, was nothing more than a trick of financial engineering – and a clumsy one at that."

to alter the corporate value of the company in question. The hypothetical case is an extreme simplification but the point is that the mere repayment of the debt causes the value of the investment (equal to the difference between the business value and the debt) to increase, despite the fact that the business value remains constant. This would allow the private equity fund to make a profit (following the divestment from this company) even if the business value has remained constant.

One observation related to the previous one is that private equity firms limit themselves to increasing the debt level of the portfolio company. Interest on the debt subscribed for the acquisition of this portfolio company would then reduce the net profits of that portfolio company, causing the portfolio company's taxable income to decrease with a consequent tax benefit and that workers feel pressure to work more efficiently, also in the face of lower remuneration precisely because of the reduced profitability of the portfolio company. All this would result in a transfer of wealth from taxpayers and workers to the coffers of private equity firms and, in some cases, of their investors[91].

In particular, skeptics note that, after the acquisition of a portfolio company, private equity firms do not seem to undertake particular activities. They would simply participate, through their representatives, in the meetings of the board of directors of the portfolio company, to seek a potential buyer of the portfolio company and, finally, to sell the portfolio company to the best bidder.

However, the limited sequence of activities reported by the critics is explained, and is perfectly consistent, with the economic model of private equity: Private equity firms - unless the management of the portfolio company is inadequate - offer generous incentive plans to the management to align the economic interests of management with the achievement of positive results by the portfolio company. In particular, private equity firms provide support and advice in the most significant corporate transactions (for example acquisitions, loans or recapitalisations) without, however, taking part in the retail management of the portfolio company which remains delegated to the management of

91 GREENWOOD D. J. H., *Looting: the puzzle of private equity*, in *Brooklyn Journal of Financial and Commercial Law*, vol. 3, 2008, p.124.

the portfolio company[92]. This explains why private equity firms are keen to emphasize their role as advisors and supporters, not antagonists, of management[93].

Excessive indebtedness: Another applicant criticizing private equity notes that private equity firms would (opportunistically) take over debt levels of portfolio companies, thus creating financial funding to make payments to private equity firms in the form of dividends, commissions or various service fees[94]. The excessive indebtedness of the portfolio companies would make them fragile, to the point that they would be more susceptible to the risk of bankruptcy, with an increase in social costs (for example if it is necessary to proceed with collective layoffs of the employees of these portfolio companies or resort to use of social safety nets).

The majority economic literature, however, believes that portfolio companies subject to acquisition by leveraged buy-outs by private equity funds have no greater probability of bankruptcy than other companies whose level of debt is comparable[95]. On the contrary, private equity firms would facilitate and speed up the debt restructuring process in the event of

---

92 CHEFFINS B. & ARMOUR J., *The Eclipse of Private Equity*, in *ECGI – Law Working Paper*, n. 082/2007, 2007, p.30. DE FONTENAY E., *Private Equity Firms As Gatekeepers*, op.cit., p.125.

93 KLAUSNER M., *Institutional Shareholders, Private Equity, and Antitakeover Protection at the IPO Stage*, in *University of Pennsylvania Law Review*, vol. 152, 2003, p.755 ss.

94 SUROWIECKI J., *Private Inequity*, in *The New Yorker*, 30 January 2012, http://www.newyorker.com/magazine/2012/01/30/private-inequity. DE FONTENAY E., *Private Equity Firms As Gatekeepers*, op.cit., p.127.

95 HOTCHKISS E. S., STRÖMBERG P. & SMITH D. C., *Private Equity and the Resolution of Financial Distress*, in *ECGI - Finance Working Paper*, n. 331/2012, 2012, according to which: "Controlling for leverage, PE-backed firms are no more likely to default than other leveraged loan borrowers. […] Taken together, our results suggest that PE investors do not exacerbate the risk of financial distress, and when defaults do occur, resolve the distress more efficiently than other firms." WILSON N. & WRIGHT M., *Private Equity, Buy-Outs and Insolvency Risk*, in *Journal of Business Finance & Accounting*, vol. 40, n. 7-8, 2013, pp.949-990. BORELL M. & TYKVOVA T., *Do Private Equity Investors Trigger Financial Distress in Their Portfolio Companies*, in *Journal of Corporate Finance*, vol. 18, n. 1, 2012, pp.138-150. DEMIROGLU C. & JAMES C. M., *Lender control and the role of private equity group reputation in buyout financing*, in *Journal of Financial Economics*, vol. 96, 2010, pp.306-330.

the insolvency of the portfolio company[96]. It was also observed that the level and the indices that measure the portfolio company's debt do not allow the risk of bankruptcy to be identified or quantified ex ante[97]. Finally, some authors show that, in the context of leveraged buy-outs with high debt, the net effect between the increase in the target company's business value and the cost of any financial failure is positive[98].

Reduction in employment levels: Some authors note that the profits of private equity firms derive from the reduction of fixed costs following the reduction in employment levels and that the rate of layoffs at portfolio companies is higher than that relating to comparable companies[99]. There are, however, authors who reach opposite conclusions[100] or conclude that private equity interventions have no

---

96 HOTCHKISS E. S., STRÖMBERG P. & SMITH D. C., *Private Equity and the Resolution of Financial Distress*, in *ECGI - Finance Working Paper*, n. 331/2012, 2012, p.30.

97 WILSON N. & WRIGHT M., *Private Equity, Buy-Outs and Insolvency Risk*, op. cit., p.978, according to which: "Of particular note is the fact that debt to total assets and its year on year changes are not significant in distinguishing buyouts that fail from non-fails."

98 ANDRADE G. & KAPLAN S., *How costly is financial (not economic) distress? Evidence from highly leveraged transactions that became distressed*, in *Journal of Finance*, vol. 53, 1998, p.1461 ss., according to which: "[T]his paper studies a sample of highly leveraged transactions (HLTs) that subsequently become financially distressed. First, we estimate the effects of financial distress on value. From pre-transaction to distress resolution, the sample firms experience a small increase in value. In other words, the net effect of the HLT and distress is to leave value slightly higher. This strongly suggests that HLTs overall – those that defaulted and those that did not – earned significantly positive market-adjusted returns."

99 GOERGEN M., O'SULLIVAN N. & WOOD G., *Private Equity Takeovers and Employment in the UK: Some Empirical Evidence*, in *ECGI Working Paper Series in Finance*, n. 310/2011, 2011, p. 3, according to which: "[T]he study finds a significant decrease in employment in acquired firms in the year immediately after the completion of the IBO compared to the non-acquired firms." DAVIS S., LERNER J., HALTIWANGER J., MIRANDA J. & JARMIN R., *Private equity and employment*, in *The Global Impact of Private Equity Report 2008 – Globalization of Alternative Investments – Working Papers* (ed. by Lerner J. & Gurung A.), vol. 1, Geneva, Switzerland, World Economic Forum, 2008, p.43 ss. GOSPEL H., PENDLETON A., VITOLS S. & WILKE P., *New Investment Funds, Restructuring, and Labor Outcomes: A European Perspective*, in *Corporate Governance: An International Review*, vol. 19, n. 3, 2011, pp.276-289.

100 WRIGHT M., BURROWS A., BALL R., SCHOLES L., MEULEMAN M. & AMESS K., *The Implications of Alternative Investment Vehicles for Corporate Governance (Report prepared for the Steering Group on Corporate Governance)*, Paris, France, OECD, 2007, http://www.oecd.org/corporate/ca/corporategovernanceprinciples/3900705

significant effects on employment levels or on remuneration levels[101]. Other authors argue, however, that where there is a reduction in the employment levels of the portfolio companies of private equity funds, there is then a phase in which new jobs are created with growth rates higher than those of comparable companies[102]. However, it is not clear whether the net effect is positive and, therefore, whether the social cost of the layoffs is offset and exceeded by the social utility deriving from the alleged creation of new jobs[103].

A recent study finds that one of the best practices introduced by private equity funds is the spread of high-performance work practices (HPWP) -organizations without rigid hierarchies where employees work in teams, with greater autonomy, based on a higher level of trust and better communication- and the greater the expected time horizon of private equity investment in a portfolio company, the greater the probability that HPWPs will be introduced or enhanced in this portfolio company[104].

Profits paid by taxpayers: Another criticism of private equity is that it would opportunistically make profits payable by taxpayers thanks to the tax benefits relating to the deductibility of interest on loans for the acquisition of portfolio companies and, in some jurisdictions, to the

---

1.pdf, THORNTON P., *Inside the Dark Box: Shedding Light on Private Equity*, London, UK, The Work Foundation, 2007. AMESS K. & WRIGHT M., *Barbarians at the Gate? Leveraged Buyouts, Private Equity and Jobs*, in *Nottingham University Business School Research Paper Series*, 2007, http://papers.ssrn.com/sol3/papers.cfm?abstract_id=1034178. BRUINING H., WRIGHT M., BOSELIE P. & BACON N., *The Impact of Business Ownership Change on Employee Relations: Buy-Outs in the UK and the Netherlands*, in *ERIM Report, Series Reference n. ERS-2004-021-ORG, 2004,* http://papers.ssrn.com/sol3/papers.cfm?abstract_id=797249. BACON N., WRIGHT M. & DEMINA N., *Management Buyouts and Human Resource Management*, in *British Journal of Industrial Relations*, vol. 42, n. 2, 2004, pp.325-347.

101 AMESS K., GIRMA, S. & WRIGHT M., *What are the Wage and Employment Consequences of Leveraged Buyouts, Private Equity and Acquisitions in the UK?*, in *Nottingham University Business School Research Paper*, n. 2008-01, 2008, p.17 ss.

102 WEIR C., JONES P. & WRIGHT M., *Public to Private Transactions, Private Equity and Performance in the UK: An Empirical Analysis of the Impact of Going Private*, in *Nottingham University Business School Research Paper*, 2008, p.40 ss, http://papers.ssrn.com/sol3/papers.cfm?abstract_id=1138616.

103 DE FONTENAY E., *Private Equity Firms As Gatekeepers*, op.cit., p.128.

104 BACON N., WRIGHT M. & DEMINA N., *Management Buyouts and Human Resource Management*, in *British Journal of Industrial Relations*, vol. 42, n. 2, 2004, 325-347.

facilitated taxation of commissions on performance. As previously illustrated, the leveraged buy-out operations postulate that the acquisition of control of a portfolio company takes place through a combination of the fund's own capital and debt capital provided by third party creditors that will be repaid thanks to the portfolio company's cash flows. Interest on debt capital is at the center of criticism because their deductibility (even if partial) from the taxable income of the portfolio company would subtract resources from the Treasury for the benefit of the private equity fund. It would therefore be a transfer of wealth from taxpayers to private equity funds. The second, more technical, topic concerns the characterization of income related to the payment of performance fees: In some jurisdictions (for example in the United States) it is not taxed with the ordinary rate of business income but with the reduced rate provided for the taxation of financial annuities. The paradox identified by private equity critics is that the high profits of private equity professionals received in the form of performance fees would be taxed at a rate lower than that at which the (significantly lower) incomes of the employees of the portfolio companies are taxed. In short, private equity would benefit from tax law gaps, once again through the transfer of wealth from taxpayers to private equity funds.

The literature, to a large extent, supports the position of the critics[105] at the same time there is no lack of (dating) studies that would prove the opposite, that is, a positive net effect in favor of the tax authorities as a consequence, among other things, of the higher revenues deriving from the taxation of borne by the shareholders of the portfolio

---

105 JENSEN M. C., KAPLAN S. N. & STIGLIN L., *Effects of LBOs on Tax Revenues of the U.S. Treasury,* in *Tax Notes*, vol. 42, n. 6, 1989, 17 ss., according to which: "The analysis challenges the argument that LBOs result in net losses of tax revenues to the U.S. Treasury. Five ways are shown in which LBOs can generate incremental revenues to the U.S. Treasury: Increased capital gains taxes for shareholders; increased operating revenues; interest income earned by LBO creditors; more efficient use of capital; and asset sales triggering additional corporate taxes on the capital gains. Offsetting these incremental revenue gains are: Increased interest deductions on the LBO debt and lower tax revenues on dividends foregone. It is concluded that the U.S. Treasury's revenues from LBO firms have increased over the time period examined and that policies that restrict LBOs likely will reduce future tax revenues received by the Federal government." RENNEBOOG L.D.R., SIMONS T. & WRIGHT M., *Why do public firms go private in the UK?*, in *Journal of Corporate Finance*, vol. 13, n. 4, 2007, p.611 ss.

companies and the creditors of the portfolio companies with reference to the interest paid on the loan for the acquisition of the portfolio company.

It is clear that this is a tax policy issue and as such must be left to the legislator. However, it should be noted that it seems legitimate to benefit from tax-efficient structures, the point to be clarified is whether private equity creates or transfers value.

Low returns: The literature on the return on private equity funds is, once again, uneven. Some authors note that the returns of private equity funds are significantly and consistently positive and at least equal to or higher than the returns offered by the capital markets for investments in listed companies with risk profiles comparable to the portfolio companies of the funds in question[106].

Other authors, on the contrary, observed that the average return of private equity funds would be lower than the average return offered by the capital markets for investments in listed companies with risk profiles comparable to the portfolio companies of the funds in question, or slightly higher than the returns of reference but only gross of commissions, charges and other costs borne by investors[107]. Part of the literature offers as an explanation of this anomaly, in addition to the irrationality of some

---

106EWENS M., JONES C. M. & RHODES-KROPF M., *The Price of Diversifiable Risk in Venture Capital and Private Equity*, in *Oxford Journals – The Review of Financial Studies*, vol. 26, n. 8, 2013, p.31 ss. LOPEZ DE SILANES F., PHALIPPOU L. & GOTTSCHALG O., *Giants at the Gate: On the Cross-Section of Private Equity Investment Returns*, in *EDHEC Working Paper*, 2011, p.31 ss. VON DRATHEN C. & FALEIRO F., *The performance of leveraged buy-out-backed IPOs in the UK*, in *London Business School Working Paper*,2007, p.29 ss. CASELLI S, GARCIA-APPENDINI E. & IPPOLITO F., *Explaining Returns in Private Equity Investments*, in *CAREFIN Working Paper*, n. 15/09, 2009, p.18 ss.. GROH A. & GOTTSCHALG O., *The risk-adjusted performance of US buy-outs*, in *HEC Working Paper*, 2006, p.27 ss. CAO J. & LERNER J., *The Performance of Reverse Leveraged Buyouts*, in *NBER Working Paper*, n. 12626, 2006, p. 21 ss. KAPLAN S. & SCHOAR A., *Private Equity Performance: Returns, Persistence, and Capital Flows*, in *The Journal of Finance*, vol. LX, n. 4, 2005, 1821 ss.

107 PHALIPPOU L., *Beware of Venturing into Private Equity*, cit., 164 ss. GOTTSCHALG O., *Private Equity and Leveraged Buy-outs*, op.cit., p.49 ss. DRIESSEN J., LIN T. & PHALIPPOU L., *Estimating the Performance and Risk Exposure of Private Equity Funds: A New Methodology*, in *NETSPAR Discussion Paper*, n. 23, 2007, p.23ss. GOTTSCHALG O., PHALIPPOU L. & ZOLLO M., *Performance of Private Equity Funds: Another Puzzle?*, in *INSEAD-Wharton Alliance Center for Global Research & Development Working Paper Series*, n.2004/82/SM/ACGRD6,2004, p.27ss.

investors, the opacity with which the costs and commissions are communicated by private equity firms to investors in private equity funds[108].

Finally, some authors have observed a positive correlation between the level of experience of the private equity firm and the returns of the private equity fund[109].

3.1.3. Positive remarks: (i) Superior corporate governance; (ii) profitability increase; and (iii) greater technological innovation

Private equity advocates respond to criticism with two types of arguments: With the first, they aim to scale back or reverse the problems identified by private equity detractors (for example with reference to the relationship between debt and bankruptcy risk of portfolio companies or to the alleged reduction in employment levels), while with the second type of arguments, they enhance some of the alleged virtues of private equity, as briefly illustrated below[110].

Superior corporate governance of portfolio companies. The economist Michael Jensen theorized in 1989 the superiority of the corporate governance model introduced by private equity funds in its portfolio companies because it would allow to mitigate agency costs[111]

---

108 PHALIPPOU L., *Beware of Venturing into Private Equity*, op.cit.,p. 164 ss.

109 JELIC R. & WRIGHT M., *Exits, performance, and late stage private equity: The case of UK management buy-outs*, in *European Financial Management*, vol. 17, 2011, p.573 ss. DILLER C. & KASERER C., *What Drives Private Equity Returns?– Fund Inflows, Skilled GPs, and/or Risk?*, in *European Financial Management*, vol. 15, n. 3, 2009, p.664 ss. LJUNGQVIST A., RICHARDSON M. & WOLFENZON D., *The Investment Behavior of Buyout Funds: Theory and Evidence*, in *ECGI – Finance Working Paper*, n. 174, 2007, p.29 ss. KNIGGE A., NOWAK E. & SCHMIDT D., *On the Performance of Private Equity Investments: Does Market Timing Matter?*, in *Journal of Financial Transformation*, vol. 16, 2006, p.129 ss. WRIGHT M., JELIC R. & SAADOUNI B., *Performance of Private to Public MBOs: The Role of Venture Capital*, in *Journal of Business Finance & Accounting*, vol. 32, n. 3-4, 2005, pp.643-682. CUMMING D. & WALZ U., *Private Equity Returns and Disclosure around the World*, in *LSE RICAFE – Working Paper*, n. 9, 2004, p.26 ss.

110 DE FONTENAY E., *Private Equity Firms As Gatekeepers*, op.cit.,p. 129.

111 In the economic literature, "agency costs" means the total of costs incurred by the principal to mitigate the risk of opportunistic behavior of the agent, for example, "surveillance costs" and incentives to guide behavior of the agent and the "obligation costs" to insure and hold the principal indemnified in the event that the agent

resulting from the separation between ownership (of shareholders) and control (of management) in companies with a broad shareholder base[112]. In particular, the pressure of the debt - contracted on the occasion of a leveraged buy-out - on management, would induce management to manage the portfolio company in order to maximize cash flows and increase the value of the company, under penalty of insolvency and the consequent bankruptcy of the portfolio company and, therefore, the loss of corporate positions by management. It is precisely the pressure of debt that spurs management to manage the portfolio company efficiently avoiding waste and mitigating the typical agency costs of companies where control and ownership are separate. In other words, leverage would have a disciplinary effect on management.

Furthermore, to ensure greater alignment of management's interests with those of private equity firms, private equity firms usually require that management invests its capital in portfolio companies and that this investment is of a significant amount so as to feel that it has interests at stake (for a similar reasoning in the relationship between limited partners and general partners with reference to direct investment in a private equity fund)[113].

Increase in profitability of portfolio companies. Most authors seem to agree that in the period immediately following the entry of the private equity fund into the capital of a portfolio company, that portfolio company generally shows financial and operational improvements

---

implements opportunistic conduct to the detriment of the principal. For further information see: JENSEN M. C. & MECKLING W. H., *Theory of the Firm: Managerial Behavior, Agency Costs and Ownership Structure*, in *Journal of Financial Economics*, vol. 3, n. 4, 1976, pp.305-360.

112 JENSEN M., *Eclipse of the Public Corporation*, in *Harvard Business Review*, 1989. Thus, the economist Adam Smith illustrated the conflict between shareholders and directors: "The directors of such [joint-stock] companies, however, being the managers rather of other people's money than of their own, it cannot well be expected, that they should watch over it with the same anxious vigilance with which the partners in a private copartnery frequently watch over their own. Negligence and profusion, therefore, must always prevail, more or less, in the management of the affairs of such a company." See: SMITH A., *Wealth of Nations*, Washington, USA, Thrifty Books, (reprint) 2009.

113 KAPLAN S. & STRÖMBERG P., *Leveraged Buyouts and Private Equity*, in *Journal of Economic Perspectives*, vol. 23, n. 1, 2009, p.130 ss.

(compared to the period prior to the entry of the fund equity investments in the capital of this portfolio company)[114].

The research also seems to support that portfolio companies (whose control was acquired through leveraged buy-outs by private equity funds) would obtain better economic results than comparable companies, even in times of recession. The above seems consistent with the efforts to rationalize, reduce costs and improve efficiency, typically required by the private equity fund to manage the portfolio company[115].

It is, however, unclear whether and to what extent the positive results are those of operational improvements or a mere reduction in costs (for example as a result of collective staff layoffs). In the latter case, it is not said that there is a positive net economic effect: The social costs deriving from the dismissal of workers could well exceed the utility

---

114FRONTIER ECONOMICS, *Exploring the impact of private equity on economic growth in Europe*, London, UK, Frontier Economics Ltd, 2013, p.32 ss. ACHARYA V.V., GOTTSCHALG O. F., HAHN M. & KEHOE C., *Corporate Governance and Value Creation: Evidence from Private Equity*, in *The Review of Corporate Finance Studies*, vol. 26, n. 2, 2013, pp.368-402.GUO S., HOTCHKISS E. & SONG, W., *Do buy- outs (Still) create value?*, in *Journal of Finance*, vol. 66, 2011, pp.479-517. BOUCLY Q., THESMAR D. & SRAER D., *Leveraged buy-outs – evidence from French deals*, in *The Global Economic Impact of Private Equity Report 2009 – Globalization of Alternative Investments– Working Papers* (ed.by Gurung A. & Lerner J.), vol. 2, World Economic Forum, 2009, pp.47-64. CRESSY R., MUNARI F. & MALIPIERO A., *Playing to their strengths? Evidence that specialization in the Private Equity industry confers competitive advantage,* in *Journal of Corporate Finance,* vol. 13, n. 4, 2007, pp.647-669. HARRIS R., SIEGEL D.S. & WRIGHT M., *Assessing the impact of management buyouts on economic efficiency: plant-level evidence from the United Kingdom,* in *The Review of Economics and Statistics,* vol. 87, 2005, pp. 148-153. *AMESS K., The effects of management buy-outs and on firm-level technical efficiency: evidence from a panel of UK machinery and equipment manufacturers,* in *Journal of Industrial Economics,* vol. 51, 2003, pp.35-44. BRUINING H. & WRIGHT M., *Entrepreneurial orientation in management buyouts and the contribution of venture capital,* in *Venture Capital: An International Journal of Entrepreneurial Finance,* vol. 4, 2002, pp.147-168. AMESS K., *Management buy-outs and firm-level productivity: evidence from a panel of UK Manufacturing Firms,* in *Scottish Journal of Political Economy,* vol. 49, 2002, pp.304-317. SMART S. B. & WALDFOGEL J., *Measuring the effect of restructuring on corporate performance: the case of management buy-outs,* in *Review of Economics and Statistics,* vol. 76, 1994, pp.503-511. OPLER T. C., *Operating performance in leveraged buy-outs,* in *Financial Management,* vol. 21, 1992, pp.27-34.

115WILSON N., WRIGHT M., SIEGEL D. & SCHOLES L., *Private equity portfolio company performance during the global recession*, in *Journal of Corporate Finance*, vol. 18, n. 1, 2011, pp.193-205.

deriving from the greater profitability of the portfolio company. Furthermore, it is not clear whether the claim for greater profitability of the portfolio companies following a private equity intervention is lasting and sustainable in the medium/long term.

Greater technological innovation: Some authors have examined patents registered by portfolio companies whose control was acquired through leveraged buy-outs by private equity funds and concluded that the average value of these patents, due to the number of subsequent citations, is greater than the average value of patents registered by other comparable companies but without the support of a private equity fund. This would seem to support a positive correlation between private equity and the registration of more valuable patents, thanks to a higher research and development activity[116].

It has also been observed that, in some industrial sectors, € 1 of private equity investments in a portfolio company can have an impact up to nine times greater, expressed on the basis of the number of registered patents, of € 1 of investments other than private equity[117] (although the relationship between patents and economic growth is not clear, technological innovations are generally protected by patents and this means that the number of registered patents is a valid index of the ability to create technological innovation and therefore economic growth)[118].

116FRONTIER ECONOMICS, *Exploring the impact of private equity on economic growth in Europe*, op.cit., p.40.
117 FRONTIER ECONOMICS, *Exploring the impact of private equity on economic growth in Europe*, op.cit., p.24 ss. LERNER J., STRÖMBERG P. & SØRENSEN M., *Private equity and long-run investment: the case of innovation*, in *The Global Impact of Private Equity Report 2008 – Globalization of Alternative Investments – Working Papers* (ed.by Lerner J. & Gurung A.), vol. 1, Geneva, Switzerland, World Economic Forum, 2008, pp.27-42.
118FRONTIER ECONOMICS, *Exploring the impact of private equity on economic growth in Europe*, op.cit, p.24 ss. POPOV A. & ROOSENBOOM P., *Does private equity investment spur innovation? Evidence from Europe*, in *European Central Bank Working Paper Series*, n. 1063, 2009.

More generally, other authors have observed a positive correlation between private equity interventions and innovation[119] as well as an increase in the number of applications for patent registration[120].

3.1.4. Conclusions reached by the majority doctrine and limits of published research

The review and analysis of the literature relating to the economic impact of private equity shows that, according to the majority doctrine, private equity has produced higher returns for investors in private equity funds, generated profits for private equity firms, favored managerial, operational and innovation improvements of portfolio companies and, overall, it is a phenomenon with a positive net economic effect, that is, private equity creates value[121].

However, the conclusions reached by the literature must be contextualized in light of some limits relating to the quantity and quality of the underlying data as well as the analysis of methodologies adopted, as illustrated below.

First of all, the research conducted by the authors focused on private equity operations carried out in the United States or the United Kingdom (also due to the greater development of the market in these geographical areas and, probably, the greater openness of local operators

---

119 POPOV A. & ROOSENBOOM P., *On the real effects of private equity investment – Evidence from business creation*, in *European Central Bank Working Paper Series*, n. 1078, 2009, pp.30-32.

120 UGHETTO E., *Assessing the contribution to innovation of private equity investors: a study on European buyouts*, in *Research Policy*, vol. 39, 2010, pp.126-140.

121 DE FONTENAY E., *Private Equity Firms As Gatekeepers*, op.cit., p.133. KAPLAN S. & STRÖMBERG P., *Leveraged Buyouts and Private Equity*, op.cit., p.143, according to which: "The empirical evidence is strong that private equity activity creates economic value on average." FRONTIER ECONOMICS, *Exploring the impact of private equity on economic growth in Europe*, op.cit., p.50. HENDERSON M. T. & EPSTEIN R. A., *Introduction to 'The Going Private Phenomenon: Causes and Implications'*, in *The University of Chicago Law & Economics – Olin Working Paper*, no. 430, 2008, p.5, according to which: "[T]he overall picture […] of private equity is positive and promising, but complex and nuanced." BERNSTEIN S., LERNER J., SØRENSEN M. & STRÖMBERG P., *Private Equity and Industry Performance*, in *NBER Working Paper*, n. 15632, 2010, p.23, according to which: "[T]he key results are, first, that industries where PE funds have invested in the past five years have grown more quickly, using a variety of measures."

to share data and information which otherwise would not be accessible to the public). Although there is no shortage of works whose research perimeter extends to the entire territory of the European Union, a first limitation of the research in question is that the results achieved in them may not be relevant outside the United States or the United Kingdom, respectively (both common law countries that differ, for example, from the civil law countries of continental Europe).

The researchers conducted analyzes and verified economic models based on public information and data made available - on an exclusively voluntary basis - by the private equity industry. It cannot be excluded that the data made available constitute an incomplete statistical sample or, worse, representative only of the best results obtained by the operators.

Much research was conducted in the period prior to the "sub-prime" mortgage crisis of 2007-2008 in a context characterized by the absence of a specific regulatory framework for private equity. It remains to be seen whether and what results can be confirmed in the light of the different context, certainly more complex and regulated, formed after the aforementioned crisis.

Private equity includes a variety of investment techniques and objects, but most research seems to have focused on the effects of leveraged buy-outs. The results must therefore be taken into consideration in the light of this specific context and cannot be generalized without further checks.

Some research has been commissioned and financed by trade associations of private equity firms: It cannot be excluded that the results observed in such research represent a partial picture or, worse, that their objectivity is compromised.

3.2. Economic impact of private equity on the debt capital market

As illustrated above, the literature on the economic impact of private equity has focused on measuring the results recorded by private equity investments in terms of profitability for investors in private equity funds and for the private equity firm, as well as management improvements, operational and in the field of innovation of the portfolio companies subject to investments by private equity funds.

An innovative interpretation of the economic impact of private equity in which portfolio companies, debt capital markets and the role of private equity[122] have recently been put forward. The thesis is that private equity firms would create value by facilitating the meeting between the demand (by their portfolio companies) and the offer of loans (by third party creditors, for example banks). This thesis postulates that: (i) There are agency costs in the debt capital market and, in particular, that there are risks of adverse selection (ex ante opportunism of the debtor) and moral hazard (ex post opportunism of the debtor) that the third party creditors would not be fully able to control; (ii) private equity firms have incentives to mitigate the aforementioned agency costs with reference to their portfolio companies; and (iii) private equity firms are effectively able to mitigate the aforementioned agency costs.

3.2.1. Agency costs in the debt capital market

In the debt capital market (i.e. in the corporate finance market) there are agency costs that originate from at least two circumstances:

(i) information asymmetries between the management of the financing company/debtor and the third party lender/creditor, which give rise to the problem of "adverse selection;" and (ii) limited control power of the third creditor over the management of the debtor company, which gives rise to the problem of "moral hazard."

The economic theory of agency costs postulates that the management of a company has more and more information than any creditor of that company, also with reference to the companies obliged to communicate relevant information to the public (think, for example, of the obligation for listed companies to disseminate, without delay, price sensitive information) and that the creditors' control over management cannot be complete and perfect.

Adverse selection means the risk that, before the loan is disbursed, the opportunistic behavior of the debtor companies leads to a sub-optimal selection of debtors by third party creditors. The third creditors, not being

122 DE FONTENAY E., *Private Equity Firms As Gatekeepers*, op.cit., p.115 ss.

able to distinguish between good debtors and bad debtors, will offer loans at conditions calculated on the basis of the average qualities of the debtors present on the market at a given moment[123]. This will represent an advantage for bad debtors and a disadvantage for good debtors, consequently good debtors will tend not to underwrite loans, while bad debtors will tend to take on loans for amounts higher than those they would have access in the absence of information asymmetries[124]. As the average quality of the debtors decreases, the creditors will require that the conditions of the loans be adjusted in pejus for the debtors. This adjustment will ensure that other good debtors do not take out loans, contributing to the further twisting of the negative spiral described here[125]. It follows that good debtors will receive fewer loans (or lesser loans) and on worse terms than the loans and conditions that would be available in the absence of information asymmetry between creditors and debtors[126].

Moral hazard means the risk that, after the disbursement of the loan, the opportunistic behavior of the debtor company favors the shareholders at the expense of third party creditors. The conflict between shareholders and social creditors is the result of the different rights and expectations that each group has on the assets of the debtor company: Creditors are entitled only to the payment of their credits (in addition to interest, if any), while the members benefit (indirectly and without limits) of increases in value of the company net of payables to social creditors; both groups are shown only for the capital, respectively, lent or

---

123 DE FONTENAY E., *Private Equity Firms As Gatekeepers*, op.cit., p.140. TIROLE J., *The Theory of Corporate Finance*, Princeton, USA, Princeton University Press, 2006. CHOI S., *Market Lessons for Gatekeepers*, in *Northwestern University Law Review*, vol. 92, n. 4, 1998, p.934 ss.

124 WHITEHEAD C. K., *The Evolution of Debt; Covenants, the Credit Market, and Corporate Governance*, in *The Journal of Corporation Law*, vol. 34, n. 3, 2009, pp.664-666. DE FONTENAY E., *Private Equity Firms As Gatekeepers*, op.cit., p.141.

125 HEALY P. M. & PALEPU K. G., *Information asymmetry, corporate disclosure, and the capital markets: A review of the empirical disclosure literature*, in *Journal of Accounting and Economics*, vol. 31, 2001, p.408.DE FONTENAY E., *Private Equity Firms As Gatekeepers*, op.cit., p.141.

126 AKERLOF G. A., *The Market for "Lemons:" Quality Uncertainty and the Market Mechanism*, in *The Quarterly Journal of Economics,* vol. 84, n. 3., 1970, pp.488-500. *DE FONTENAY E., Private Equity Firms As Gatekeepers,* op.cit., p.141.

conferred[127]. This explains why shareholders may have diverging interests from creditors, especially in the event that the net financial position is negative: In this case, while creditors will have an interest in preserving the existing corporate assets, shareholders - in the assumption that after payment there would be nothing left of social debts - they could have an interest in making the company undertake particularly risky activities. Like the problem of adverse selection, the problem of moral hazard also causes creditors to adjust the conditions of the loans (in pejus for the debtors) and therefore the debtor companies obtain loans on lesser terms[128].

The debt capital market has developed some procedural and contractual practices to mitigate the risks of opportunistic behavior of debtors. In particular, to mitigate the risk of adverse selection, creditors carefully examine their debtors, especially from a financial and legal point of view, performing a verification activity similar to the due diligence activities carried out on the occasion of corporate acquisitions and creditors develop relationships long-term with its debtors; while the risk of moral hazard is typically mitigated by means of direct control of the debtor's management and activities and by the do-or-not-do obligations foreseen in the loan agreement (for example, the obligation to inform the creditor in advance regarding extraordinary corporate transactions or the obligation not to contract further financial payables beyond a certain threshold without the prior consent of the creditor)[129].

The procedural and contractual practices referred to above were born and developed in the context of traditional type loans and with a simple structure, usually having a single creditor. The debt capital market is far more complex today. For obvious reasons of risk diversification, it is more and more frequent that the loan is shared between several credit institutions that act in consortium with each other so that the exposure (in

---

127 ROCK E. B., *Adapting to the New Shareholder-Centric Reality*, in *University of Pennsylvania Law Review*, vol. 161, 2013, p.1927. MYERS S. C., *Determinants of Corporate Borrowing*, in *Journal of Financial Economics*, vol. 5, n. 2, 1977, pp.147-175.

128 DE FONTENAY E., *Private Equity Firms As Gatekeepers*, op.cit., pp.141-142.

129 DE FONTENAY E., *Private Equity Firms As Gatekeepers*, op.cit., p.143.

the event of the debtor's insolvency) is distributed[130]. This division can also take place after the disbursement of the loan thanks to the development of an increasingly liquid secondary market for loans[131]. A further factor of complexity has been the spread of credit securitization operations, through which pecuniary loans are sold in bulk to a company vehicle specifically created for the transformation of these credits into securities negotiable on the financial market[132].

The new financing techniques, including syndicated loans and credit securitisations, have allowed the debt capital market to develop considerably and facilitate access to debt. However, they undermined the traditional creditor-debtor relationship, weakening the procedural and contractual remedies that had been devised by the operators of the financing market to mitigate agency costs. It is easy to understand that in a syndicated loan between numerous credit institutions, each institution will have weak incentives to monitor the debtor because the monitoring costs would be direct costs for that institution while the benefits would be shared among all the other credit institutions[133]. Thus, the higher the level of syndication, the lower the incentives of creditors to monitor the debtor. In addition, syndicated loans present the typical criticalities of multi-party contracts, for example the risk of being held hostage by the opportunistic behavior of (even only) one of the parties should the consent of this party be necessary for the modification of the terms of the loan. It is precisely to remedy this risk that in practice loan agreements provide for greater flexibility (in favor of the borrower). However, this flexibility can lend itself to the borrower's abuse and opportunistic behavior. Therefore, while

---

130 In such cases the loan is called "syndicated loan." There is an "organizing bank" which coordinates the negotiations and the consortium of "participating banks" for financing. In more complex loans, the "organizing" bank is assisted by an "agent bank" which, after the signing of the loan agreement, deals with the administrative aspects (for example communications, collections, payments).

131 DE FONTENAY E., *Private Equity Firms As Gatekeepers*, op.cit., p.143.

132 BARTLETT R. P., *Taking Finance Seriously: How Debt Financing Distorts Bidding Outcomes in Corporate Takeovers*, in *Fordham Law Review*, vol. 76, 2008, p.2013 ss.

133 SHIVDASANI A. & WANG Y., *Did Structured Credit Fuel the LBO Boom?*, in *The Journal of Finance*, vol. 66, n. 4, 2011, pp.1315-1316. OLSON M., *The Logic of Collective Actions: Public Goods and the Theory of Groups*, Cambridge, USA, Harvard University Press, 1965.

the benefits of syndication of loans are risk diversification in favor of creditors and greater ease of access to the debt capital market in favor of debtors, syndication reduces at the same time the incentives to monitor the activities of the debtor and the resort to stringent contractual obligations to do (or not to do) in loan agreements; this exacerbates the risk of adverse selection and moral hazard of the debtor[134].

3.2.2. Incentives of the private equity firm to mitigate agency costs

Private equity firms are regular operators in the debt capital market and negotiate loans whose amounts are significant. It is these two circumstances that incentivize private equity firms to make their portfolio companies act as good debtors. In particular, to maintain their reputation in the market, private equity firms have incentives to mitigate the risk of adverse selection, acting as intermediaries for the certification of the quality of their portfolio companies, and to mitigate the risk of moral hazard, acting as intermediaries for monitoring the management of its portfolio companies.

Obviously private equity firms do not negotiate loans on their own but act in the name and on behalf of their (numerous) portfolio companies[135]. Furthermore, the amount of loans underwritten by portfolio companies tends to be higher than the amount of loans that these portfolio companies would underwrite in the absence of the support of private equity firms. In particular, the economic literature notes that the ratio between debt and equity of the portfolio companies supported by private equity firms tends to be higher than the corresponding ratio in the absence of support from private equity firms for at least two reasons: The first is that the higher level debt represents a competitive advantage for private equity firms as it allows them to offer a higher price for the acquisition of the portfolio company and thus beat the competition in the corporate

134DE FONTENAY E., *Private Equity Firms As Gatekeepers*, op.cit., p.148. DEMIROGLU C. & JAMES C. M., *Lender control and the role of private equity group reputation in buyout financing*, op.cit., pp.306- 310.

135IVASHINA V. & KOVNER A., *The Private Equity Advantage: Leveraged Buyout Firms and Relationship Banking*, in *The Review of Financial Studies*, vol. 24, n. 7, 2011, p.2466 ss.

control market of portfolio companies[136]; the second is that the current market terms relating to the remuneration of private equity firms create incentives to maximize the debt/equity ratio of the portfolio company[137]. For these reasons, it is noted that portfolio companies supported by private equity funds tend to underwrite loans for the maximum amount obtainable regardless of operational needs. Furthermore, consider that private equity firms usually organize multiple private equity funds and that each fund controls different portfolio companies. It can therefore be concluded that private equity firms are regular operators in the financing market because they operate there more frequently and for greater amounts than each portfolio company considered individually. As regular operators in the debt capital market, private equity firms have a strong reputational incentive to negotiate in good faith with third party creditors and ensure that their portfolio companies do the same. In fact, third party creditors will have the opportunity to observe the behavior of the portfolio company over time and this behavior will have (even if only partially) an impact on the terms and conditions of the loan contracts which will subsequently be signed by other portfolio companies attributable to the same private equity firm.

Well, the incentives and interests of the portfolio company management could diverge from the incentives and interests of the private equity firm: Generally, management - unlike the private equity firm - does not run particular reputational risks towards operators of the debt capital market because it does not it is a regular operator in this market and does not move large volumes of debt capital. The interest of the management will therefore be short-term and aimed at obtaining the financing of its portfolio company at the best conditions, while the interest of the private equity firm will be to avoid any form of misconduct of the portfolio

136BARTLETT R. P., *Taking Finance Seriously: How Debt Financing Distorts Bidding Outcomes in Corporate Takeovers*, in *Fordham Law Review*, vol. 76, 2008, pp.1975-2026.

137The greater the use of leverage, the greater and more numerous are the investments in portfolio companies for the private equity fund and therefore the expected returns for the private equity fund. AXELSON U., STRÖMBERG P. & WEISBACH S., *Why Are Buyouts Levered? The Financial Structure of Private Equity Funds*, in *The Journal of Finance*, vol. 64, n. 4, 2009, p.1555. DE FONTENAY E., *Private Equity Firms As Gatekeepers*, op.cit., p.150.

company or of the management because potentially harmful to the future relations with creditors (on the assumption that the benefits obtainable through incorrect conduct in the short term are less than the damages that the private equity firm would suffer in the long term)[138]. It is precisely this divergence between incentives and interests that makes private equity firms valid intermediaries for monitoring their portfolio companies and, therefore, for reducing agency costs[139].

Borrowing the expression from game theory, it has been observed that the interactions of private equity firms with the creditors of their portfolio companies are comparable to repeated games. The above analysis would be different if the interaction were comparable to a single and non-repeatable game, because in that case also the private equity firm would have short-term interests and incentives[140].

This point can be illustrated with the following example from De Fontenay (2013): Assume that (i) a portfolio company, whose business value is originally € 100 million, is acquired through leveraged buy-outs from a fund of private equity with € 20 million of equity capital and € 80 million of financing by third parties; (ii) following an extraordinary event, the business value of this portfolio company has decreased from € 100 million to € 80 million; and (iii) at this point the portfolio company is practically on the verge of insolvency having sufficient resources to repay only the financing for the acquisition (assuming, for simplicity, that no interest has accrued and there are no commissions payable). It is also assumed that the portfolio company has two options: (a) Repay the € 80 million loan to creditors; or (b) undertake a project that with a 10% probability will increase the business value to € 500 million but that with a 90% probability will reduce the business value to € 0. Option (a) is preferable for creditors who would receive a refund of their credit, but very bad for the private equity fund which would see the value of their investment in the portfolio company zero. Option (b) is bad both for creditors (who risk not receiving full repayment of their loan) and for the

138 DE FONTENAY E., *Private Equity Firms As Gatekeepers*, op.cit., p.153.
139 COFFEE J. C., *Gatekeeper Failure and Reform: The Challenge of Fashioning Relevant Reforms*, in *Boston University Law Review*, vol. 84, 2004, pp.301–64.
140 GREENWOOD D. J. H., *Democracy and Delaware: The Mysterious Race to the Top/Bottom*, in *Yale Law and Policy Review*, vol. 23, 2005, pp.381-454.

portfolio company which should expect a reduction in the business value to € 50 million[141] and the onset of the state of insolvency. However, from the point of view of the private equity firm, option (b) is preferable to option (a) because, although the value of the investment in the portfolio company is more likely to be zeroed, with a slight probability the private equity firm will be able to recover the value of your investment and even get profits. If the interaction between private equity firm and creditors took place only once (i.e. if it was a single game, in the jargon of game theory) the dominant strategy of private equity firm would always be to maximize short-term profits and private equity firm would choose option (b); if, on the other hand, the private equity firm expects to interact again (or for an indefinite number of times) with creditors in the debt capital market, it would have an incentive to select option (a) because -although losing with certainty the value of your investment- would maintain its reputation in the financing market without prejudice to the possibility of taking out new loans on favorable terms[142]. In addition to the above, the financing market is extremely concentrated, therefore the number of creditors with which the private equity firms interact is small[143]. This reinforces the incentives of private equity firms to ensure the good conduct of their portfolio companies (but, of course, the intensity with which these incentives motivate private equity firms will also depend on the ability and probability that creditors find out if and when private equity firms act opportunistically)[144].

3.2.3. Ability of the private equity firm to mitigate agency costs

After illustrating the reasons why private equity firms have incentives to mitigate agency costs in the context of loans to their portfolio companies, it seems useful to analyze whether private equity firms have the capacity to mitigate these agency costs.

---

141 The expected business value is calculated as follows: 0.1 * € 500 million + 0.9 * € 0 = € 50 million.
142 DE FONTENAY E., *Private Equity Firms As Gatekeepers*, op.cit., p.155.
143 HIVDASANI A. & WANG Y., *Did Structured Credit Fuel the LBO Boom?*, op.cit., p.1306.
144 DE FONTENAY E., *Private Equity Firms As Gatekeepers*, op.cit., p.155 ss.

From the creditor's point of view, the problem of the adverse selection of a debtor is divided into three questions: A first question concerns the probability that, in the absence of specific knowledge relating to a potential debtor, this potential debtor is of poor quality (therefore the percentage statistics of bad debtors among potential debtors); a second question concerns the determination of the real quality of the potential debtor, assuming that the debtor shares data and information in full transparency (but this also depends on the quality of the information available and the ability to make accurate forecasts); a third question concerns the risk that the potential debtor is not reliable and, therefore, makes false statements or fails to provide relevant information.

The private equity firms, as illustrated below, are able to intervene positively on each of the three issues indicated above, in order to mitigate the risk of adverse selection. Specifically, with reference to the risk that the portfolio company is a bad debtor, it is plausible to assume that private equity firms have the ability to identify and select higher quality companies and exercise this ability: The main activity of private equity firms is precisely identify, analyze and select portfolio companies with high potential for their investments. As for the difficulty of determining the real quality of the potential debtor, consider that, before each investment, the private equity firm analyzes the (potential) portfolio company from multiple points of view, also thanks to repeated meetings with the management of the (potential) portfolio company and external consultants[145]. Furthermore, once the acquisition of the portfolio company has been completed, the private equity firm has full access to information and full control over the management of the portfolio company, thus ensuring that the portfolio company does not make false statements or fails to provide relevant information[146].

---

145 For example: Strategic, financial consultants, tax and legal consultants, industrial experts, etc. SPINDLER J. C., *How Private Is Private Equity, and at What Cost?*, in *The University of Chicago Law Review*, vol. 76, 2009, pp.309-332.

146 MASULIS R. W. & THOMAS R. S., *Does Private Equity Create Wealth? The Effects of Private Equity and Derivatives on Corporate Governance*, in *University of Chicago Law Review*, vol. 76, 2009, pp.223-224. DE FONTENAY E., *Private Equity Firms As Gatekeepers*, op.cit., pp.159-160.

As for the problem of moral hazard, private equity firms - unlike any creditor - have full control and ability to intervene on their portfolio companies, thus being able to prevent and prevent the management of their portfolio companies from carrying out opportunistic acts to the detriment of creditors (this would undermine the reputation of the private equity firm and the possibility that it will be able to enter into financing contracts on favorable terms in the future). Furthermore, from the creditors' point of view, the portfolio companies supported by private equity firms have an additional competitive advantage compared to the other debtors: In the event of financial failure, the private equity firms would have the economic resources as well as the technical and relational knowledge to remedy to this crisis situation, also through a further capital injection in the portfolio company[147].

From the above it follows that the (indirect) investment of the private equity firm in a portfolio company would act as a filter and would have a sort of certification value of the qualities of this portfolio company and of the monitoring that the private equity firm will exercise on this portfolio company.

3.2.4. First conclusions on the role of private equity in the debt capital market and critical remarks

In support of the argument that private equity firms play a positive role in the debt capital market, recent empirical research has shown a positive correlation between the reputation of private equity firms (measured as a function of the number of years of activity in the private equity sector and the total amount of the assets entrusted to them under management) and more favorable conditions in the financing of the portfolio companies of funds attributable to these private equity firms[148].

147HOTCHKISS E. S., STRÖMBERG P. & SMITH D. C., *Private Equity and the Resolution of Financial Distress*, op.cit.,pp. 23-24. DE FONTENAY E., *Private Equity Firms As Gatekeepers*, op.cit., p.160 ss.

148DEMIROGLU C. & JAMES C. M., *Lender control and the role of private equity group reputation in buyout financing*, op.cit., p.306 ss. DE FONTENAY E., *Private Equity Firms As Gatekeepers*, op.cit., p.165 ss. DE MAESENEIRE W. & BRINKHUIS S., *What drives leverage in leveraged buyouts? An analysis of European leveraged buyouts' capital structure*, in *Accounting & Finance*, vol. 52, n. 1s, 2012, pp.155-182.

This result is surprising if one considers that neither private equity firms nor private equity funds are (legally) liable in the event of insolvency of the portfolio company for debts entered into in the context of a leveraged buy-out. It therefore seems plausible that creditors take into account the reputation of private equity firms in providing loans to the portfolio companies of these private equity firms and that these private equity firms exercise preventive controls and continuous monitoring on their portfolio companies in order to mitigate the risks of opportunistic behavior to the detriment of creditors, just as illustrated in the thesis according to which private equity firms would choose long-term strategies aimed at mitigating the risks of opportunistic behavior of their portfolio companies in damage to creditors.

Other empirical research has shown that the greater the frequency with which a private equity firm interacts with a creditor, the better the financing conditions offered by that creditor to portfolio companies attributable to that private equity firm[149]. These results also seem consistent with the thesis that private equity firms would choose long-term strategies aimed at mitigating the risks of opportunistic behavior of their portfolio companies damaging creditors.

After illustrating the nature and characteristics of agency costs in the debt capital market, the incentives for private equity firms to mitigate the risks of opportunistic behavior, the ability of private equity firms to mitigate the aforementioned agency costs and the results of the empirical research, it seems legitimate to conclude that private equity firms can and, to some extent, play a positive role in the debt capital market by facilitating the matching of supply and demand of loans to their portfolio companies[150]. In light of the context outlined, it is easy to appreciate that this role represents, for private equity firms, a significant competitive advantage compared to other competitors in the corporate control market.

---

149 IVASHINA V. & KOVNER A., *The Private Equity Advantage: Leveraged Buyout Firms and Relationship Banking*, in *The Review of Financial Studies*, vol. 24, n. 7, 2011, pp.2462-2498; DE FONTENAY E., *Private Equity Firms As Gatekeepers*, op.cit., p.165 ss.

150 DE FONTENAY E., *Private Equity Firms As Gatekeepers*,op. cit., pp.115-189.

However, it should be noted that the literature has also put forward alternative hypotheses that could explain why private equity firms are able to obtain financing on more favorable terms for their portfolio companies.

A first alternative hypothesis is based on the observation that the secondary market of loans to portfolio companies of private equity funds is significantly more liquid -it is therefore easier for creditors to transfer financial instruments or securities representing their credit rights- compared to the secondary market for other types of loans. The increase in the demand for loans for private equity operations in the secondary market would cause them to be taken out on more favorable terms (for portfolio companies) in the primary debt capital market[151].

A second alternative hypothesis is that creditors would offer financing on more favorable terms for portfolio companies of private equity firms because these creditors would aim to offer other services (for example financial advice in extraordinary operations) to these portfolio companies or private equity firms and so collect the most lucrative commissions provided for these other services[152].

A third alternative hypothesis is that private equity firms are able to obtain loans on more favorable terms for their portfolio companies thanks to greater negotiating power, derived from better knowledge of the market (by negotiating a significant number of financing contracts, private equity firms they know which terms and conditions reflect market terms and conditions) and derived from the greater ability to negotiate sophisticated financing contracts (being more familiar with financial engineering techniques)[153].

Furthermore, the keeping of the thesis in question - namely that private equity firms create value by facilitating the meeting between the

---

151 DE FONTENAY E., *Private Equity Firms As Gatekeepers*, op.cit., pp.166-167.
152 IVASHINA V. & KOVNER A., *The Private Equity Advantage: Leveraged Buyout Firms and Relationship Banking*, op.cit., p.2462. ACHARYA V. V., FRANKS J. & SERVAES H., *Private Equity: Boom and Bust?*, in *Journal of Applied Corporate Finance*, vol. 19, n. 4, 2007, pp.44-53. DE FONTENAY E., *Private Equity Firms As Gatekeepers*, op.cit., p.168.
153 KAPLAN S. & STRÖMBERG P., *Leveraged Buyouts and Private Equity*, op.cit., pp.140-141. AXELSON U., JENKINSON T., STRÖMBERG P. & WEISBACH S., *Borrow Cheap, Buy High?*, in *The Journal of Finance*, vol. 68, n. 6, 2013, pp.2223–2267.

demand for loans, by their portfolio companies, and the offer of loans, by third party creditors, for example banks- lends itself to at least two critical observations which will be illustrated below.

A first critical point regards the use of debt capital raised by portfolio companies. It has been shown that, thanks to the support and role played by the private equity firm, the portfolio company is able to take out a loan on more favorable terms (for example at a lower interest rate or for a higher amount) than conditions that it could have obtained without the support of the private equity firm. This, on the one hand, allows portfolio companies to access the financing market with greater agility, on the other, it helps creditors to use their capital usefully. However, it remains to be seen what the fate of these debt capital is. It is not possible to exclude that these capitals are used sub-optimally and opportunistically distracted in favor of the private equity firm (for example in the form of commissions or fees to the advisory company, the general partner or to other subjects attributable to the private equity firm). In short, the role of private equity in facilitating the meeting between the demand (by its portfolio companies) and the offer of loans (by third party creditors, for example banks) does not imply that the capital obtained by the portfolio companies are used in an optimal way that adds value.

A second critical point concerns the possibility that the scope of the alleged reputational risk for the private equity firm is overestimated. In the first place, it could happen that the private equity firm evaluates the reputational damage resulting from an opportunistic behavior lower than the benefit deriving from this one (also as a consequence of the so-called "overconfidence"[154] documented by behavioral finance). Secondly, when we talk about private equity firms, we are actually referring to the private

---

154 "Overconfidence" means the predisposition to a cognitive error, represented by the natural tendency of man, on the one hand, to overestimate his own skills and abilities and, on the other hand, to underestimate the volatility of random events. For further information see: BARBERIS N. & THALER R., *A Survey of Behavioral Finance*, in *Handbook of the Economics of Finance* (ed.by Constantinides G., Harris M. & Stulz R.), Amsterdam, Holland, Elsevier, 2013. On the role of overconfidence in decision making in general, see: KAHNEMAN D. & LOVALLO D., *Timid Choices and Bold Forecasts: A Cognitive Perspective on Risk Taking*, in *Management Science*, vol. 39, n. 1, 1993, pp. 17-31. On the impact of overconfidence on managers, see ex multis, BEN-DAVID I., GRAHAM J. R. & CAMPBELL R. H., *Managerial Overconfidence and Corporate Policies*, in *NBER Working Paper*, n. 13711, 2007.

equity professionals who are part of it. There are no published studies that relate the relationship between mobility (which could be significantly high) of these professionals to other jobs and the reputation of a private equity firm. However, it does not seem possible to exclude that within the private equity firm there are professionals with strong incentives to adopt opportunistic behaviors aimed at achieving short-term benefits, especially in the presence of strong mobility among private equity professionals. Strict provisions in the contracts for hiring staff from private equity firms and the presence of internal control and risk monitoring offices can mitigate but not eliminate the risk that excessively risky or potentially prejudicial conduct for the private equity firm will be assumed.

CHAPTER 3

Application of private equity in the infrastructure sectors related to environmental sustainability

1. Introduction

Private equity funds mainly invested in the 80s and 90s in company restructuring, managing to easily achieve efficiency gains and, therefore, profitability. As we have already analyzed in the previous chapter. Today all this has become more difficult, because the sector is experiencing strong competition, which has limited its returns, and undergoes the slowdown of the financial markets and the world economy, which began in the summer of 2007, with the credit-crunch[155].

---

155 The term credit crunch indicates a significant drop (or sudden tightening of conditions) in the supply of credit at the end of a prolonged expansion period, capable of accentuating the recession. Credit crunch usually occurs at the end of the expansion phase, when central banks raise interest rates in order to cool the expansion and avoid inflation risk, prompting lenders to raise their interest rates and closing the access to credit for those who cannot afford the expense. In other cases, it may happen that, in the wake of bank failures and withdrawal of liquidity, banks apply a credit closure to avoid bankruptcy themselves. As a result of the credit squeeze, bankruptcies of both banks and debtor firms and families may occur. The missed payments that are created, and the possible bankruptcies, translate into foreclosures of the mortgaged assets to guarantee the loans, and an increase in the properties of the banks. Non-performing loans expose credit institutions to a similar risk of foreclosures or bankruptcy. The properties acquired remain within the sphere of credit institutions, taking into account that the main lenders of these institutions are possibly subjects that carry out the same type of credit activity. Where the greatest liquidity injection comes from a central bank, if it is controlled by the same banks to which it lends money, the business risk of the credit institutions is reduced even in the event of strong insolvencies of their customers. In the event of bankruptcy of an institution, which at the same time controls its main creditor, this may not exercise the guarantees provided by law for its protection. The credit crunch occurred particularly during the 1929 crisis. Some economists said that the subprime mortgage crisis could lead to a new credit crunch, in 2007.

A response to overcome the slowdown that the buyout has undergone, due to the subprime crisis of the last decade, constitutes the action of private equity in the sector of economic infrastructures and in that of sustainable finance, as a consequence of the new needs of institutional investors chasing safe and real investments, in a world seared by derivative finance.

This chapter therefore investigates the characteristics and developments of the infrastructure world, characterized by an important growth in investments in project finance. The infrastructures, due to the effect of important global dynamics (demographic development, growth in the needs of emerging countries, scarcity of natural and energy resources) are the engine of competitiveness of the country systems, which make it the center of their economic policies.

The evolution expected in the most dynamic infrastructural sub-sectors connected to the theme of environmental sustainability: Water, energy and transport is then described.

The characteristics of the infrastructure investment and the reasons for a renewed interest of institutional investors for this form of investment, now defined as a new and autonomous asset class, are also studied. Interesting news in the panorama of infrastructure financing, which we focus on, is the birth of infrastructure funds, or private equity funds specialized in the sector.

After investigating their growth dynamics, they hint at their intersection with the problems of climate change, with the development of the so-called carbon funds sector, a moment of transition towards investments in the world of environmental sustainability.

The problems of climate change and the security of energy supplies, combined with the need to respond to an increase in energy demand from developing countries and from a longer-lived world population, have in fact forced the financial system to pay greater attention to the issues environmental sustainability, which, from a constraint, in a few years have become a strong economic opportunity.

The ratification of the Kyoto Protocol and the subsequent development of carbon finance have given way to the development of sustainable finance and what we call here "clean economy." In a few years, from a small market with European relevance, the Emission Trading Scheme (ETS) born in Kyoto, has allowed the creation of markets for the exchange of emission certificates now starting all over the world. At the Bali conference in December 2007, after years of skepticism for some (especially the United States), the world took the path of environmental sustainability, further strengthened by the elections of the "green" Barack Obama as the new President of the United States, and the Copenhagen Summit at the end of 2009 "should" mark the birth of a global carbon market. Thus a new industrial sector emerged, that of clean technologies, "infrastructures" that allow the production of energy without greenhouse gas emissions.

At market level, this statement is made evident by the development of infrastructure funds, carbon funds and SRI (sustainable responsible investment), which have become the subject of enormous investment demand from institutional and private investors. Finally, the major institutional investors (i.e. pension funds, foundations and insurance companies), in search of long-term and low-risk social assets, have become the main supporters of the investment funds dedicated to financing sustainable investments and the clean economy.

In this new scenario, as we will see later on the world of private equity, in its role of intermediation between public institutional investors (pension funds, foundations) and private (wealthy people, investment banks, insurance etc.) and the business world, will play a leading role in driving the growth of "green" companies. In a recent meeting with Silicon Valley entrepreneurs, the nobel prize winner Al Gore stated that the green revolution represents, in fact, precisely the solution to the financial crisis.

2. Private equity in infrastructure financing

In recent years the world has witnessed an intense phase of transformation of economic systems. Its primary role was played by the phenomenon of privatizations, aimed at seeking greater efficiency in the sectors traditionally managed by the state and reducing the high level of public debt.

With the privatization processes, all countries have disciplined competition and privatized the management of many utilities, in the production and administration of energy and other main public tariff services (water, transport, networks, waste, etc.).

Privatizations brought businesses and businesses previously managed and financed by the state to the market, expanding the space for private finance. The high risk associated with many initiatives, the significant capital necessary for their financing and the need to put together different entrepreneurial experiences, meant that the formula of the so-called "project company" was established for the realization of new investments and with it the technique of project finance[156]. With project finance there has been a real conceptual revolution in the evaluation of an economic initiative: In short, the focus has shifted from the financial strength of the promoter to the goodness of the project idea.

Following the privatization phase, in recent years a key element in the development of the so-called public-private partnerships (PPPs) on international financial markets is that of the provision of infrastructures.

While historically businesses and states have won economic competition with their competitors, through the levers of natural resources, capital and/or technologies, now that natural wealth represents an ever lesser advantage than in the past, product technologies are moving with great rapidity and the capitals are now free to move, the competition becomes more a match between "country-systems," which is played on all the conveniences to invest in a given area rather than another.

The comparative advantage is realized in the presence of clear and advantageous "rules of the game;" in the characteristics of elements of general competitiveness and in the presence of so-called externalities, attributable to the efficiency of bureaucracies and the presence of modern and functional infrastructures.

New infrastructures mean better services, and therefore improving the quality of life of citizens: In a final analysis, from a political point of view, they can also affect the stability of the electorate. And the policy of the developed countries is strongly aware of this. The importance of

---

156 Project Financing means the method of "financing a project with legal and economic autonomy - pursued by the promoters also in order to limit its impact on their financial statements - granted on the basis of the cash flow made in the future by the investment and the entrepreneurial skills of the managers of the initiative."

infrastructures and their contribution to the development of companies is evident in history.

In developed countries, economic infrastructures thus represent the most important table on which to play the game of international competition. For this reason, all countries have sought new ways to finance and manage them, stimulating the capital and entrepreneurial skills of individuals and contributing to the international development of infrastructure finance.

2.1. The development of infrastructure project finance

In a simple way, an infrastructure can be defined as "any system that connects A with B," or as a "permanent asset that a company requires to facilitate the ordinary operation of its economy." The infrastructures are divided into two categories: "Economic infrastructures" which generally include the sectors of transport (highways, airports, ports, railways), energy (distribution and generation of gas and electricity), water (irrigation and water treatment) and communications (communication towers, satellites, fiber optic networks), and "social infrastructures" which include schools, hospitals, prisons.

Infrastructures are not an end but a means of ensuring the supply of goods and services that promote growth, well-being and quality of life. To date, precisely because of the large size of the projects and the huge investments needed, the infrastructure has historically been financed, built, owned and managed by the state. In the modern era, however, due to reduced public budgets and increased needs of a population continuously growing all over the world, these investments are almost always accompanied by the formation of the so-called public private partnerships (PPP), or contractual systems in which a public service or a private initiative is financed and made operational through a partnership between the public administration and one or more private companies.

PPPs initially grew following the problems arising from the levels of public debt, which rapidly increased with the macroeconomic problems that occurred in the 70s and 80s, starting from the Anglo-Saxon experience.

In the midst of a strong economic downturn in England, the British Conservative government of John Major introduced in 1992 the Private Finance Initiative (PFI), the first global program born with the aim of encouraging the development of the PPP, with the main objective of reduction in the volume of public debt.

At that time the British government was caught between the demand for public investment and the limited capacity resulting from the current taxation to meet this demand: The fiscal deficit was growing and the private sector investment in the public was seen as a way of improving public finances[157].

Tony Blair's subsequent Labor government, elected in 1997, continued with the PFI, placing greater emphasis on achieving high economic efficiency in public investment, the so-called "value for money." More than 700 projects worth £ 46 billion had been completed by 1992, and PFI's projects accounted for between 10 and 15% of the total investment in public infrastructure. In addition, there was an important pipeline of around 200 projects worth around £ 26 billion until 2010.

Numerous governments have followed Anglo-Saxon experience and have adopted PFI-based programs. To date, PPP-PFI-type infrastructure finance transactions are structured all over the world, with a predominant weight in Europe. At world level, the main financing technique with which PPPs are implemented, especially the infrastructural ones, is project financing. According to Yescombe[158] project finance "is a long-term debt collection method for the development of large projects through the use of financial engineering, which depends on a detailed assessment of construction, operational and commercial risks, and on their subsequent allocation between investors, creditors, and other parties through specific contracts."

Project finance "is a long-term debt collection method for the development of large projects through the use of financial engineering,

---

157 CLARK,G.L. & ROOT,A., *Infrastructure shortfall in the United Kingdom: the private finance initiative and government policy*, in *Political Geography* , vol.18, 1999, pp. 341-365.

158 YESCOMBE E.R., *Principles of Project Finance*, Academic Press, 2002. NEVITT P., *"Project Financing,"* Euromoney, 2000. IMPERATORI G., *"Il project financing: una tecnica, una cultura, una politica,"* Milan, Italy, Il Sole 24 Ore, 1995.

which depends on a detailed assessment of construction, operational and commercial risks, and on their subsequent allocation among investors, creditors, and other parties through specific contracts."

Several studies have shown that the use of project finance positively affects the investment decisions of a private action, while Modigliani and Miller in their "irrelevance proposition" point out that the financing methods do not change the value of an investment[159]. Esty, for example, points out that in some cases financial structures matter and that the economic growth of project finance is a consequence of the fact that this technique reduces the net financing cost of infrastructures[160].

The usefulness of project finance for the realization of complex infrastructure projects is in fact evident, especially in a time of recession - delicate for the budgets of states, where infrastructures represent the place where a country's economic policy can converge with the market of capital for the achievement of social objectives. In fact, project finance guarantees the realization of efficient investments, with the use of limited public resources, a good rate of return for private investors, and being a source of diversification with respect to the stock markets, it allows the stabilization of the returns of institutional investors.

In this evolution, the private equity industry has already begun, for reasons of economic opportunity and for the needs of its institutional investors, to specialize in infrastructure and renewable energy, through the infrastructure funds, which we will discuss later. This trend is expected to continue in the coming years, as industrialized countries, as we will see, will need to improve their infrastructure to compete in a world that suddenly found itself with limited and expensive natural resources (water, energy, environmental quality, raw materials). Throughout this process, climate change, and the global policies that are rapidly emerging, will have the role of drivers for a "hunt" for renewable energy infrastructures and sustainable investments, which has already begun and is starting the birth of a new paradigm of development.

---

159 SBREALEY S., MYER R.A., SANDRI A.F., *Principi di finanza aziendale*, McGraw-Hill, 1999.
160 ESTY B. C., *The economic motivations for using Project Finance*, in *Mimeo*, 2003.

2.1.1. The sub sectors: Water, energy and transport infrastructures

Let us now briefly examine what happens and will happen in the infrastructural sectors linked more to the theme of environmental sustainability: Water, energy and transport.

a) Water infrastructures: The water sector is already today the symbol of the importance of the world of infrastructures in the coming years, because it summarizes the new context, characterized by strong population growth and increasingly limited natural resources, in which the world it is quickly setting up.

Water is essential for our life. We need it for personal use, to grow food, and to theoretically produce everything we need to live. However, this resource is expected to become even more scarcely available. The world water market is vast, but the bulk is concentrated in the "supply" and "wastewater treatment" sectors.

The development of the water market is driven by four mega-trends, or explosive growth in the world population, aging of existing infrastructures, demand for better quality water and, above all, climate change. These trends will increase the need to manage existing resources more efficiently than in previous years. It is clear that, as pressure increases on the planet's limited resources, consumers will become more aware of the fact that water (already defined today, blue gold) is a precious asset that needs to be managed in a sustainable way.

For example, the U.S. Environmental Protection Agency[161] estimated that costs for coping with sewage spills, repairing or replacing existing transportation and installing new sewage systems accounted for 52% of the $ 271 billion necessary to meet the American needs related to waste water treatment infrastructures.

Globally, it has been estimated that investments in water infrastructure and wastewater infrastructure in terms of utilities amounted to $ 100 and $ 104 billion respectively[162].

---

161 OUDEJANS L., *Report on the 2016 U.S. Environmental Protection Agency (EPA) International Decontamination Research and Development Conference*. U.S. Environmental Protection Agency, Washington, DC, EPA/600/R-17/174, 2017.

162 LAWLESS H.T., HEYMANN H., *Sensory evaluation of food: principles and practices*, 2nd edition, New York, USA, Springer, 2010.

There is now a growing acceptance of the fact that water must be associated with a price tag that accurately reflects its vital role for our life, especially when the water resources available for individual use continue to decrease in a world characterized by a growing population but with constant resources.

b) Energy infrastructures: The liberalization of the electricity and gas market, attention to global warming, energy prices and growing demand in emerging economies are shaping the scenario in which utilities operate in the world, bringing companies of the sector to shift the focus towards clean, renewable and distributed energy.

Electricity companies are responsible for increasing energy efficiency in the coming years, both on the demand and on the supply side, to reduce the environmental impact. At the same time, these companies are facing increased competition and volatility in prices and greenhouse gas emissions from plants with a high intensity of harmful emissions.

At the same time, they will have to face persistent opposition to the implementation of large infrastructure projects, in a sector where the ability to support long-term value creation will depend on access to new generation infrastructures.

The competitiveness of companies will depend on the implementation of strategies that seek opportunities in a scenario characterized by climate change and which therefore mitigate environmental risks.

From a scenario point of view, the World Energy Outlook 2019 "the current financial crisis is expected to have no repercussions on long-term investments, but may however cause delays in the completion of ongoing projects, especially in the electricity sector."

It is interesting to note that just over half of the world's energy investments, scheduled for the 2007-30 period, will only serve to maintain current capacity, "as most of the world's current infrastructure for oil, gas, coal and electricity supplies it will have to be replaced by 2030."

The link between investments in energy infrastructures and climate change is important: "To provide an adequate framework on the conditions that will govern future investments for energy infrastructures, it is essential that negotiations for an international agreement on climate change are concluded quickly and that the related implications on national policies are assessed quickly."

Specifically, 800 million Euros have been allocated in the EU to be divided over 14 Community projects ranging from the electricity to the gas sector. Resources will be provided by the Connecting Europe Facility (CEF), the European support program for trans-European infrastructures. Of the 800 million, over 500 will go to projects on electricity and smart grids, including the construction of a Baltic electricity synchronization system. Each project was chosen because it is capable of increasing competitiveness, improving the security of energy supply and contributing to sustainable development and environmental protection[163].

c) Transport infrastructure: In Europe, the transport sector is essential for growth and competitiveness, generating an annual turnover of around 363 billion euros (or 4.5% of the GDP) and employing more than 8.2 million people.

In the United States, according to the "Economic Impact of Infrastructure Investment" report, produced in July 2017 by J.M. Stupak for the Congressional Research Service, considering the 126 billion dollars that Congress has allocated for infrastructure in just one year, half went to finance transportation projects. In addition, he claims that financing the debt infrastructure of the United States will have a multiplier effect. Building debt railways and bridges acts as a sounding board: The Congressional Budget Office has calculated that a 100 billion increase in publicly funded investments would increase GDP by 20 billion in the short term. Hence the indication, entrusted to the United States Congress, to beat the path of public investment to be financed by debt, not only for the modernization of infrastructure works but also for the economic development of the country.

2.1.2. The characteristics of infrastructure investments

Infrastructure investments are characterized by some peculiarities, which make them interesting to particular types of private investors.

---

163 CANALE ENERGIA, *Dall'UE 800 mln di euro per infrastrutture energetiche prioritarie. I finanziamenti rientrano nel Connecting Europe Facility*, 29 January 2019.

Let's start by stating that, in recent years, investments in infrastructure have generally been characterized by an overall higher performance than that of the equity markets.

One of the most important indices in the world of infrastructures, UBS Global Infrastructure, with those obtained from the world equity benchmark MSCI World, the former was clearly greater[164]. The need for essential services such as roads, water, electricity and gas is such that, during the last financial crisis, which occurred between 2000 and 2003, while the MSCI World Index lost around 30%, the UBS Infrastructure Index grew by 17%[165].

In summary, the infrastructures guarantee higher returns, a greater distribution of dividends, and a lower volatility of the stock market. A further important feature of infrastructure investments is their being strongly linked to the trend of "real" interest rates. In fact, infrastructures are generally underperforming in a scenario of increasing interest rates and outperforming in situations of decreasing rates. As a result, returns on infrastructure investments are unrelated to the world of bonds.

2.1.3. The development of private equity funds for infrastructure

The growth dynamics of the infrastructure sector and the characteristics of this type of investment have created a great deal of attention in the business and financial world, and in particular in the world of private equity.

In addition to the huge market of listed infrastructures, numerous specialized financial vehicles were born: Private equity funds for infrastructures, better known as infrastructure funds. The latter can be seen as an evolution of project financing and private equity, which meet here in the realization of long-term social and economic objectives. Infrastructure funds are financial vehicles that operate with a private equity approach, but take on a connotation of hybrid investment, as they operate in a sector with a high social value.

---

164 WALKER, S.T., *Understanding Alternative Investments: Creating Diversified portfolios that ride the wave of investment success,* New York, USA, Palgrave Macmillan, 2014.

165 *Ibidem.*

They specialize on a single investment class (e.g. airports) or on multiple infrastructure sectors, characterized by monopoly situations, on a regional or global scale. The main investors in infrastructure funds are the institutional ones which, as already seen, find in this asset class essential characteristics such as the stability of the cash flows, low volatility and good inflation-related returns.

In addition to this, by investing in infrastructure funds rather than in individual infrastructure stocks, investors have access to the manager's managerial skills in selecting and managing assets.

Wanting to make a bit of history, the idea of creating closed-end funds, specialized in infrastructure, was from the Australian Macquarie Bank, the first to recognize the opportunities present in the sector of infrastructure for the private sector. Already in 1996 the Australian bank began, in fact, to form funds specialized in infrastructures to acquire and finance assets all over the world, arriving in 2007 to manage a portfolio of 102 assets in 25 countries, although the phenomenon has developed strongly only in the last few years. In particular, the sector has seen the explosion of financial operators who have established their infrastructure funds, and the weight of private equity on the total volume of global investments in infrastructure has exceeded 50% of the total for a value of around 50 billion dollars[166].

The concentration of the financial mass was even greater if we considered the operators rather than the individual funds, with Macquarie in the first place to which were attributable 15 billion euros, 28.6% of the total. Next came the American insurance - financial giant AIG (which was then hit drastically by the 2008 financial crisis) which has an investment target of five billion euros, and finally Goldman Sachs with GS Infrastructure Fund, launched in 2006, with amounting to 4.8 billion euros.

Many other investment banks launched in 2008 their own infrastructure fund. Among them, Carlyle set up a team dedicated to the infrastructure sector and then formed, together with Riverstone, a $ 685 million fund dedicated to the renewable energy sector.

---

166 HILL K.F., *Infrastructure funds on the rise*, January/February 2008, www. renewcanada.net ReNew Canada.

General Electric and Credit Suisse announced the birth of a billion dollar joint venture called Global Infrastructure Partners in 2008.

In operation, the infrastructure funds have the same characteristics as a classic private equity fund, described previously, with an SGR, in the role of general partner, which has the task of managing investments deriving from limited partners.

Wanting to define the types of investment, in the world of infrastructure the distinction between private equity and venture capital can be well described between brownfield investments (existing infrastructures) and greenfield (new infrastructures).

In fact, between the two types of investments there are the same differences that are found between private equity and venture capital, in terms of technological risk profiles, in the predictability of cash flows, in the time of realization.

The operation of these funds is "simple:" After careful selection, they invest in long-term operations, low risk, stable and predictable returns, in regulated sectors. One of the advantages of these operators consists, as seen in the case of classic private equity funds, in being able to borrow in multiples of their capitalization, and consequently have the possibility to increase (even tenfold, during the boom phase of 2007) the investments compared to the initial capital.

Since the possibility of indebtedness is precluded to pension funds, foundations or insurance companies, infrastructure funds become very advantageous, offering the opportunity to improve the profitability and diversification of investments.

In addition to classic institutional investors, infrastructure funds see funds that manage state assets as strong investors, such as the case of the famous Americans "State of NY" and "State of California" (which managed over $ 100 billion in 2007) at Canadian and French Caisse des Depots, to the German Kfwv, to the Spanish Echoes up to the Italian Cassa Depositi e Prestiti. Infrastructure Funds, in general, do well for the private sector, bringing dividends of all respect to those who subscribe them.

To give some examples, the 2006 balance sheet of the Tata Infrastructure Fund in Mumbai showed a gross profit of 62% and the Sunduran BNP Paribas Select Midcap Fund an even of 92%. Over the next three years, the sector has seen a huge acceleration: The development of the so-called "asset packagers" (primarily the Australian Macquarie) has led to strong competition on the pricing of the works, with a lowering of the level of risk, and the subsequent recall of huge economic resources by pension funds.

Precisely this presence of extra-liquidity then created an excessive imbalance between demand and supply of assets in which to invest, with the consequent growth of multiples, and the subsequent sector bubble, which burst with the crisis of the financial and credit markets, to which a slight drop in yields followed, which in 2007 was around 10-15%, from a survey by Probitas Partners[167].

In truth, the sector is experiencing a stalemate, in 2008, induced by the current financial crisis. Today, after ten years of crisis, infrastructures demonstrate a crowded space with a lot of fund managers competing for deals in all regions globally. And infrastructure isn't created out of thin air (unlike IT start-ups, for example) hence supply of good deals is growing much slower than demand. Demand is there, because limited partners throughout the world finally appreciate benefits of investing in infrastructure (meaningful return with protected downside and low correlation to other assets - very good combination).

Speaking about the US market, historically US institutions (such as public pension plans) were comfortable with traditional private equity and energy-focused private equity. Infrastructure asset class was somewhat overlooked in the United States. While Western Europe loved infra for its risk-return profile, the US apparently was finding infra to be a bit too boring. In recent years US has been catching up actively but still it is clear that perception or risk in the US is a bit different. What would be considered value add infra in Europe, would be routinely treated as "core"/ "core-plus" in the US. Also US pension plans are in love with energy-

---

167 PROBITAS PARTNERS, *"Investing in Infrastructure Funds,"* September 2007. "The survey was carried out in the spring of 2007 with the aim of investigating the views and prospects on investments in infrastructure funds, contacting around 1500 institutional investors and receiving responses from 114 managers of public and private pension funds, funds, family offices, foundations and endowments, consultants, insurance companies and other agencies. In addition, dozens of telephone interviews were conducted with the most important and most active institutional investors to obtain a better understanding of the trends noted in the survey."

related infrastructure so in recent years some asset types that were historically considered "traditional private equity" for years (merchant power plants, merchant oil and gas pipelines, even refineries) are now being pushed into infrastructure territory (with IRRs falling correspondingly). To give an idea, infra private equity fund in the US can buy into a construction of a merchant (i.e. no government subsidies or guarantees) gas power plant or even wind park. In Europe, infra funds would only consider it if it is already operating and has some sort of subsidy (capacity payments or else). There are of course exceptions here and there but this should give us a general idea of Europe vs US dynamics. Generally, in the US the borderline between energy-focused private equity and infra private equity is sometimes blurred. Such names as ArcLight Capital Partners, Energy Capital Partners - these are on the border between infra private equity and energy private equity.

Within infrastructure, financial investors can be broadly divided into two groups: Fund managers and institutional investors (latter being pension plans, insurance companies and sovereign wealth funds). Until recently the infra private equity landscape was dominated by fund managers, with institutional investors supplying passive money to them. However, the trend in recent years is big institutional investors going direct - that is, building their own direct investment teams that would compete for deals with fund managers. Some (especially Canadian pension plans) are ahead of the curve and strong and experienced enough to do deals on their own. Given high quality of people and cost of capital being lower than traditional infra private equity fund, they are seen as a very serious contender[168].

2.1.4. Carbon funds and "zero-low emission" infrastructures

Carbon funds are born as a derivation of the ratification of the Kyoto Protocol, an international environmental treaty which entered into force in 2005, which started the so-called carbon finance[169], through the

168 WSO, *Overview of Infrastructure Private Equity,* 2 January 2017.

169 Carbon finance is a new branch of environmental finance, which explores the financial implications of living in a carbon-constrained world, a one in which CO2 emissions from other polluting gases are characterized by a price associated with them. Thus the general

implementation of three flexible mechanisms, with which value is finally attributed economic to the so-called "environmental externalities"[170] generated in industrial activities, subject to the setting of a system of emission quotas, at the level of industrial sectors and individual countries.

In addition to the so-called ETS (European Trading Scheme), the financial market for the exchange of emission rights, now in full growth phase, the Kyoto protocol allows a financial operator to use two other important flexible mechanisms, the CDM (Clean Development Mechanism) and JI (Joint Implementation), thus being able to buy and sell "certificates," produced in infrastructure projects, at a value defined by the financial market.

The growth of environmental policies, and the parallel development of sustainable finance, which we will analyze in the next paragraphs, see in the carbon funds places in which to combine two different sources of return, the one deriving from the investment in a classic infrastructure and the one created by the generation of "emission certificates."

In fact, carbon funds are nothing more than private equity funds for infrastructures participated by public and private investors (companies, public bodies, etc.): They are born with the main purpose of obtaining extra returns from monetary investments (equity) in zero infrastructures/low-emission achieved in developing countries and in economies in transition. These extra returns derive from the fact that the net cash flows generated by the operations of these infrastructures increase

---

term is applied to those investments in harmful emission reduction projects and to the creation of financial instruments which are marketed on the so-called carbon markets.

170 By externality is meant an effect exerted by the action of an agent, e.g. through the production or consumption of an asset, on another agent. A classic case is that of cigarette smoking. Agent A smokes a cigarette (action from which he derives pleasure), but its action generates a negative impact on agent B, which does not tolerate smoking. In other words, in the utility function of B a variable appears (the cigarette) which is under the control of agent A, the value of which is decided by agent A, regardless of the effect on B, and whose growth it destroys the utility of agent B. In this case we speak of negative externality. Other conditions of negative externality highlighted by the literature are: That externality is an unintended effect of a legitimate activity; that the agent causing the damage does not compensate the injured party. MISHAN E.J., "*Cost-Benefit Analysis: An Introduction,*" New York, USA, Praeger Publishers, 1971. BAUMOL W.J., OATES W., "*The Theory of Environmental Policy.*" Cambridge University Press, Cambridge, 1988.

thanks to the sale of the so-called "emission certificates" to the entities that finance the fund, in order to avoid higher social and financial costs deriving from their failure fulfillment of obligations deriving from Kyoto policies.

The analysis of the current use of these tools shows surprising data in terms of potential entrepreneurial development at international level for companies operating in the sector of renewable energy sources, energy efficiency and, more generally, the so-called "clean economy".

Today the carbon funds sector is still growing even though it has stalled with the subprime crisis. The total value of the global carbon market stalled at $142 billion in 2010. Suffering from the lack of post-regulatory clarity, the value of the primary CDM market fell by double-digits for the third year in a row, ending lower than it was in 2005, the first year of the Kyoto protocol. The Assigned Amount Unit (AAU) and the United States Regional Greenhouse Gas Initiative (RGGI) markets shrank as well[171].

However, the total value of the carbon market grew by 11 percent in 2011, to $176 billion, and transaction volumes reached a new high of 10.3 billion tons of carbon dioxide equivalent (CO2e). This growth took place in the face of economic turbulence, growing long-term oversupply in the EU Emissions Trading Scheme (EU ETS) and plummeting carbon prices. By far, the largest segment of the carbon market was that of EU Allowances (EUAs), valued at $148 billion. At the same time, several new domestic and regional carbon market initiatives gained traction in both developed and developing economies in 2011. Five new jurisdictions (i.e., Australia, California, Québec, Republic of Korea, and Mexico) passed legislations laying the foundation for cap-and-trade schemes. Together, these initiatives will drive substantial resources towards low-carbon investments and they have the potential to unleash a truly transformational carbon market, in support of a global solution to the climate challenge[172].

---

171 WORLD BANK REPORT, *State and trends of the carbon market 2011*, Washington DC, n.63270, 2011.
172 WORLD BANK REPORT, *State and Trends of the Carbon Market 2012*, Washington DC, n.76837, 2012.

According to World Bank significant investment in infrastructure is needed over the next years, that is around US$ 90 trillion by 2030[173].

As regards, however, the JI projects they mainly target projects related to methane and renewable energy. JI projects acting at both the international and national level. JI provides for a greater role for national authorities, and with it, creates substantial requirements for the host government in terms of capacity and institutions. Established property rights over emission reduction units as well as the system of the contract enforcement can significantly increase the willingness to invest in and ensure the IJ projects. Private sector entities are key players in JI. They will participate as investors or co-investors, project proponents and operational entities. Companies, as well as governments, require institutional capacity to carry out their IJ activities that in some cases will go beyond their normal capabilities. To maximise economic gains from the JI, it is important to develop local expertise in these new areas of economic activities. However, the number of these experts in many countries is very low[174].

2.1.5. The activity of a Carbon Fund

A carbon fund is a particular type of private equity fund: A financial container in which, while on the one hand (governments and companies from developed countries interested in reducing their carbon intensity), financial resources enter and emission certificates come out, from the other (developing countries and economies in transition, interested in accelerating their development in a sustainable way) emission certificates enter and financial resources come out.

From an investor's point of view, an investment in the equity of a CDM/JI infrastructure generally guarantees extra-profitability, compared to traditional infrastructures, which varies, depending on the technology used, from 0.5-2.5% for classic wind, hydroelectric and geothermal projects, at 3-7% for biomass projects at 5-15% for municipal solid waste treatment projects[175].

---

173 WORLD BANK, *Climate Finance*, 4 October 2019.

174 MULLINS F., *"Joint Implementation Institutions: Implementing IJ at the National Level,"* Paris, OECD, 2002.

175 WOLRD BANK REPORT, *State and Trends of the Carbon Market 2012*, op.cit.

For this reason, carbon funds become an excellent investment target for infrastructure funds, indeed they represent an evolution in the path towards the so-called clean economy, which we will discuss later.

An advanced infrastructure fund will have to invest essentially in "zero/low carbon" infrastructures, that is infrastructures which, in addition to the generation of cash flows deriving from charging, also generate cash flows deriving from the efficiency of the use of natural resources, in order to generate energy cost savings, and decreases in environmental impact/greenhouse gas emissions.

These investors will also obtain a strong diversification effect, thanks to the possibility of investing on a wide range of infrastructures (innovative/mature technologies), characterized by different investment cycles and types of risk, and achievable all over the world.

From a conceptual point of view, then, carbon funds represent a key passage for the world of institutional investors and private equity: the one that leads from the world of purely financial investments to a new way of conceiving financial activity, which draws inspiration from the theme of "environmental sustainability," to trace new long-term growth paths.

2.2. Private equity in financing environmental sustainability

After the experience gained in the infrastructure sector, private equity in the coming years will become a primary player in the development of sustainable and environmental finance, which has grown in recent years.

Indeed, the issue of environmental sustainability represents a further evolution of private equity investments, as the new social and geo-political needs and the enormous opportunities for economic and financial performance developed around the problem of climate change converge in it. Environmental protection was considered as a limit to the planet's activities and economic and social development, until the 1980s. The real breakthrough occurred in 1992, with the Rio Conference or United Nations "Earth Summit" which radically innovated the environmental policies hitherto pursued, especially with the launch of the "United Nations

Framework Convention on Change climatic," mother of the Kyoto Protocol[176].

In Rio, a common goal was established: To ensure responsible economic development, while protecting natural and environmental resources for the benefit of future generations. Subsequently, the theory of sustainable development slowly emerged. Working for sustainable development means addressing environmental issues, considering them as priority factors in the planning and execution of human activities.

In summary, it contributes to sustainable development when it is possible to produce by consuming less energy, when renewable and low environmental impact energy sources are made available and the consumption of raw materials is reduced by optimizing production cycles and reusing by-products, waste and waste. Finally, sustainable development is the one that carefully analyzes the long-term effect of human activities on the environment, when they are planned, because the way they are implemented will depend on the level of livability in future years.

In terms of investment, then, from the Rio Conference to today, a huge amount of money has been spent all over the world to prevent or reduce the environmental damage caused by human activities. Two different schools of thought followed on the type of impact of this expense.

In the United States of the 1990s, numerous studies continued to argue that environmental policies had caused the country's loss of competitiveness in the international scenario[177] while another strand of research, headed by Porter[178] asserted, instead, that environmental policies operated as a positive force guiding private companies and the whole economy towards greater competitiveness in international markets.

With the victory of Porter's thinking, which occurred during the 90s, we began to look at the environment as a driving force for the development of economies and innovation.

---

176 UN, *United Nations Conference on Environment and Development (UNCED)*, Earth Summit, 1992, available at:https://sustainabledevelopment.un.org/milestones/unced

177 JAFFE, A. B, et al, *"Environmental Regulation and the competitiveness of U.S. manufacturing: What does the evidence tell Us?,"* in *Journal of Economic Literature*, vol.33, 1995, pp. 132-163.

178 PORTER, M. "*American's green strategy*," Sci. Amer., Apr.1991, p.168.

With increasing global sensitivity to the problem of climate change, institutional investors, companies and economic operators have started to look at the environment as a potential generator of "sustainable" wealth, because they are more attentive to maintaining a trust relationship with its stakeholders (customers, suppliers, investors, civil society).

In particular, institutional investors view with great attention the opportunities deriving from the environment, intended both as a driver for the maintenance, in the coming years, of the living standards acquired by their investors, and by worker-citizens, and as an important opportunity for diversification of returns and improvement of the image of "social responsibility."

Therefore, the private equity funds, responding to the needs of their investors and the macro-agendas related to the theme of sustainability, will increasingly look to the infrastructural world in the energy sector, supporting the growth of the clean technologies industry, "a set of products, services and processes that use renewable materials and energy, greatly reduce the use of natural resources and cut or eliminate emissions and waste"[179].

Clean technologies have already started a promising new economy, which many believe as the heir to the Hi-Tech Economy, commonly called the Clean Economy. There are numerous investment funds totally dedicated to sustainable investments, which today operate mainly in the clean economy industry, directly or through specialized funds.

2.2.1. Climate change: From constraint to opportunity

Since the industrial revolution, the concentration of CO2 in the atmosphere has grown by 35% - from 280 parts per million (ppm) in 1750, to 315 ppm in 1957 to 382 ppm today.

The current concentration is the highest ever in the past 650,000 years and if the trend continues, CO2 levels could reach 550 ppm by 2050 and even 1000 ppm by the end of the century.

---

179 Definition taken from Clean Edge, a research company specialized in the sector.

In Stern Review[180],climate change is defined as "the largest market failure ever seen in history" and compared to the phenomenon of globalization, as "slow but powerful and inexorable force that changes prices and relative costs, the structures of demand, and with them the structures of the offer."

From an economic point of view, in October 2007 Lehman Brothers estimated the social cost of long-term stabilization of emissions, around a sustainable value of 450 ppm, around hundreds of billions of dollars per year[181], while the Stern report indicates a value annual average of 180 billion between now and 2050[182].

The WEO defines two alternative and improvement energy scenarios, one characterized by a CO2 concentration of 550 ppmv (550 Policy Scenario) and the other optimal at 450 ppmv (450 Policy Scenario). These scenarios, essential to avoid environmental catastrophes, above all require a strong acceleration in the production of renewable energy and in the increase in energy efficiency[183].

2.2.2. Sustainable finance and the development of the clean economy

Today's science of sustainability deals with concrete problems, such as access to clean water, the advancement of renewable energy, the mitigation of the impact of pollution on human health, food safety, the protection of bio -diversity and in general the effective use of natural and environmental resources to improve poverty conditions.

From a financial point of view, responsible investment today means the addition of environmental, social and governance analyzes (ESG analysis) to the investor's decision-making process and, in general, for sustainable business "the explicit recognition of the fact that the factors

---

180 STERN N., "*The Economics of Climate Change*," Cambridge University Press, March 2014 (online publication).

181 LLEWELLY J., *The Business of Climate Change. Challenges and opportunities*, Lehman brothers, October 2007.

182 STERN N., "*The Economics of Climate Change*," op.cit.

183 WORLD ENERGY OUTLOOK 2019, available at: https://www.iea.org/reports/world-energy-outlook-2019.

long-term environmental, social, governance, ethical and economic impact the business"[184].

This method of investment today represents an area of growing general interest as it offers long-term value creation opportunities for investors and for the whole company. Institutional investors (foundations and universities, pension funds, socially responsible investors such as mutual funds, no profits and others) have thus spread the practice of investing in assets that seek to achieve social and/or environmental and adequate financial returns together.

An important figure comes from the growing number of subscriptions to the so-called "Equator Principles"[185]: in April 2008, 60 global financial institutions had adhered to these guidelines for sustainable investments, leading to an important shift in attention towards this financial sector.

In recent years it is evident that the attention for the so-called SRIs has risen drastically all over the world, today an acronym for "sustainable and responsible investments" which EuroSif defines as follows: "SRI is a generic term for ethical investments, responsible investments, sustainable investments, and any other type of investment that combines investors' financial objectives with a focus on environmental, social and governance issues." SRI therefore means an investment process that considers the social and environmental consequences, both positive and negative, in the context of a rigorous financial analysis. The next step for Europe and the industry is to gain consensus around what are the criteria that define

184 BLOOD, D. in "*The case for sustainable business*," Gresham College, 21 January 2008.

185 The Equator Principles (EP) are a set of environmental and social benchmarks for managing environmental and social issues in development project finance globally. Once adopted by banks and other financial institutions, the Equator Principles commit the adoptees to refrain from financing projects that fail to follow the processes defined by the Principles. The Equator Principles were developed by private sector banks – led by Citigroup, ABN AMRO, Barclays and WestLB – and were launched in June 2003. The banks chose to model the Equator Principles on the environmental standards of the World Bank and the social policies of the International Finance Corporation (IFC). 60 financial institutions (April 2008) have adopted the Equator Principles, which have become the de facto standard for banks and investors on how to assess major development projects around theworld.

sustainable and responsible investing, to ensure a transparent level playing field to support future growth[186].

Today, the value of investments managed by the Investor Network on Climate Risk - INCR[187], a network of about 130 institutional investors representing more than $17 trillion in assets committed to addressing the risks and seizing the opportunities resulting from climate change and other sustainability challenges.

The socially responsible investment (SRI) market is today an important source of financing for the so-called clean economy. There are two types of socially responsible investors: Ethical and long-term investors.

The former invest in environmentally friendly companies whose products and services create a positive impact on the environment, while the latter recognize in clean technologies the place to simultaneously achieve social, environmental and financial objectives.

Although there is no official definition of clean technology, it is a technology that optimizes the use of natural resources and reduces or eliminates environmental emissions.

2.2.3. Investments in clean technologies and markets

Investments in clean technologies come from various sources: Venture capital, private equity, hedge funds, research and development, public subsidies and others.

The growth of these investments is linked to the need to drastically reduce harmful emissions in the world, through the use of low-carbon technologies. It should be noted that clean technologies are many and differ in their greater or lesser marketability.

Some are still in an embryonic phase, such as fuel cells, clean coal and biodiesel produced from cellulose, while others, such as wind and hydroelectric, have long been competitive with traditional energy sources, and others, such as solar, they will be shortly.

---

186 EUROSIF, *European SRI Study,* 2018.
187 INCR is a network of investors that promotes a better understanding of the risks and opportunities posed by climate change.

The European Emissions Trading Scheme (ETS) clearly remains the largest market, with a volume of transactions that exceeded three billion tons of CO_2 in 2018 and which is allowing the European Union to move towards the ambitious goals it has set[188].

2.3. Conclusions and outlook

This study was born with the aim of offering insights into the evolution of private equity in the worlds of infrastructure and sustainable-environmental finance. Given the complexity of such new and evolutionary themes, the discussion has remained on a conceptual level, limiting itself to providing some quantitative references that show current trends.

First of all, it is clear that, after the years of structured finance and the central role of the so-called information & communication technologies (which will continue to play an important role in the "green economy"), the next will increasingly be characterized by the return to associated finance to the development of those sectors which guarantee the real growth of economies, that is infrastructures and the environment, and will see the central role of clean technologies.

Infrastructure finance will increasingly be the place of attraction for institutional and private equity investors looking for stable and long-term returns. In real terms today, the number of fund mangers who signed the United Nations-supported Principles for Responsible Investment (PRI) grew more than 2,000 in 2018 from 1,200 in 2013. The $ 82 trillion in assets under management by these signatories increased by a compound annual rate of 19% in the same period. Of 22,000 investors worldwide, 78% know they place more emphasis on sustainability now than they did five years before, according to Schroders 2017 global investor study[189].

---

188 The 30 highest emitting power plants alone emitted in 2018, 329.2 Mt CO_2, 30% of the total EU combustion emissions in that year. The top emitting power plants are located in Poland and Germany, and burn lignite fuel. EUROPEAN ENVIRONMENT AGENCY, *Climate change mitigation. Trends and projections in Europe 2019. The EU Emissions Trading System in 2019: trends and projections*, 31 October 2019.

189 SCHRODERS, *Global Investor Study 2017. Investor behaviour: from priorities to expectations*, 2018.

In infrastructures they will find a new way of conceiving their business, no longer focused only on financial aspects but, as is rightly the case in an advanced society, above all on social and sustainability aspects. Indeed, more than 90% of the world's 250 largest companies published corporate social responsibility (CSR) or sustainability reports in 2018, compared with 45% in 2002.

The experience in the world of infrastructure will thus represent a phase of transition of institutional investors towards the growing world of sustainable and environmental finance, which will be the subject of strong attention from all economic sectors, thanks to the concurrence between the problem of climate change and the political tensions resulting from the mis-match between supply and demand for traditional energy resources and infrastructures.

This process, which is still ongoing, will finally induce the citizen-consumer to get out of the passive attitude "suffered" in the Internet age and find himself in the role of leader of a slow and inexorable social and economic revolution with a "green color:" The clean economy in fact.

In the coming years, more and more financial resources will thus move towards the world of clean technologies and the clean economy, which will allow the unrepeatable opportunity for the whole world to identify a path of fair and sustainable growth, respecting the limited natural resources, and the possibility for financial operators and companies, which will operate investment policies in environmental sustainability, to obtain extra-profitability[190], since in the meantime: Green technologies will be increasingly economically advantageous; environmental policies will go global; infrastructure demand will further increase; the consumer will make informed choices that respect the environment; politics will have to respond to these new needs. For these reasons, the future of private equity and finance is closely connected to sustainability and the environment.

However, this effort is still nascent, and some of it is simply lip service, instead of real action.

---

190 A comprehensive 2015 review by the German investment fund DWS and the University of Hamburg of more than 2,000 studies found that 63% showed a strong correlation between ESG performance and positive returns, while 10% showed a negative effect.

Impact investing, which dedicates capital to companies that generate social or environmental benefits, also is on the rise and attracting a growing number of private equity funds. What used to be the terrain of core impact investors like LeapFrog Investments or Bamboo Capital Partners now is luring some of the largest private equity funds. TPG's $ 2 billion Rise Fund 1 was the largest pool of capital dedicated to social and environmental impact when it closed in 2017[191].

Fund managers keen to adopt an environmental, social and government focus often feel confused about the right approach. One reason is that investors and the media use the labels-environmental, social and government (ESG) investing, social and responsible investing and impact investing-interchangeably, blurring the boundaries between different aims.

ESG opportunity seekers look for investment opportunities to support environmental, social or governance progress. Some work with their portfolio companies to increase their environmental or social impact, and almost all pursue investments in ESG-linked sectors such as renewables and waste management. For example, Temasek's initiatives include managing and integrating ESG factors into the investment analysis and understanding ESG risks and opportunities in the portfolio, based on defined criteria[192].

Impact investors, unlike ESG investors, invest only in assets with significant social and environmental impact. They build ESG capabilities at portfolio companies, and most develop tailored performance indicators to measure ESG impact in addition to financial returns. For example, LeapFrog Investments[193] began as an impact investment fund providing microinsurance to the poor, helping finance small business investments. Today, it focuses on financial services and healthcare in Africa and Asia and typically invests $10 million to $50 million.

Overall, ESG and impact investing can help funds stand out in a crowed market. The United Nations' Sustainable Development Goals

---

191 GANDHI V.S., BRUMME C.R., MEHTA S., "*The Rise Fund: TPG Bets Big on Impact,*" in *Harvard Business School* case 318-041, February 2018 (revised August 2019).
192 Temasek is an investment company headquartered in Singapore. It owns a $231 billion portfolio as at 31 March 2019, mainly in Singapore and the rest of Asia.
193 For further details visit the page: https://www.leapfroginvest.com/.

provides a framework with 17 clearly defined objectives, which can help funds focus on tangible ESG goals. However, to measure results, no single approach works for all funds. The criteria are different for ESG risk mitigators, opportunity seekers and impact investors.

Last but not least. Greater commitment to environmental and social goals will help private equity funds create financial returns while having a positive impact on the world.

CHAPTER 4

Comparative analysis of private equity regulation in the United States and the European Union

1. Financial crisis of 2007-2008 and G20 response

The causes (or more correctly the concauses) of the financial crisis of 2007-2008 have been the subject of in-depth studies by the economic literature and the authors seem to agree in observing that the weaknesses of the regulatory and supervisory framework of the financial sector were determining factors of the aforementioned crisis[194]. In a work of the European Commission[195] the main shortcomings have been identified as follows:

a) Inadequate macro and micro-prudential supervision and regulation: The legislators and the authorities responsible for the supervision and regulation of financial markets did not assess and react adequately to the progressive increase in risks in the market. The absence of macro-prudential supervision led to an excessive and uncontrolled growth in the assets of financial institutions and the emergence of speculative bubbles. The regulation of the financial sector was inadequate, especially where entrusted exclusively to the operators' self-regulation, because it failed to protect investors. While the major financial institutions expanded significantly beyond their national borders and the financial

---

194 CLAESSENS S., KOSE M. A., LAEVEN L. & VALENCIA F., *Financial Crises: Causes, Consequences, and Policy Responses*, Washington D.C., USA, International Monetary Fund, 2014. ROUBINI N. & MIHM S., *Crisis economics: A crash course in the future of finance*, New York, USA, Penguin Press, 2010. REINHART C. M. & ROGOFF K. S., *This time it's different: eight centuries of financial folly*, Princeton, USA, Princeton University Press, 2009.

195 EUROPEAN COMMISSION, *Commission staff working document – Economic Review of the Financial Regulation Agenda*, SWD(2014) 158 final, 2014, p.28.

markets became increasingly integrated internationally, regulatory and supervisory activities operated at the national level.

b) Financial leverage and limited ability to absorb losses: The expansion of the assets of financial institutions took place mainly thanks to the greater use of leverage (therefore the financing of third parties). At the height of the global crisis of 2007-2008 in many credit institutions the ratio between equity and assets was less than 3% (moreover, it appeared that a large part of the hybrid capital of credit institutions was of poor quality). The increase in leverage diminished the banks' ability to absorb losses, as later demonstrated during the 2007-2008 crisis.

c) Limited ability to cope with liquidity crises: Banks increasingly relied on the ability to finance their operations through interbank loans and short-term carry-overs. The temporal dissociation between loans of long and short-term made banks extremely vulnerable to sudden liquidity crises.

d) Absence of a procedure for the orderly liquidation and closure of the activities of financial institutions: There was no procedure aimed at regulating the phases and requirements necessary for an orderly liquidation and closure of the activities of a financial institution, nor were there common rules governing insolvency proceedings relating to bankruptcies of financial institutions having operations in multiple legal systems.

e) "Too big to fail" problem: It is the risk of opportunistic behavior (in particular moral hazard) of financial institutions considered too large in their own system to be deprived of public aid (also in the form of loans and capital injections) in case of risk of bankruptcy. Specifically, the risk is that these institutions have an excessive risk appetite by implicitly relying on public intervention in case of need. In addition, the institutions in question, enjoying access to loans on more favorable terms (thanks to the implicit public support) would create a competitive imbalance in the market for loans to financial institutions[196].

---

196 Recently the thesis has been put forward that "too big to fail" regulatory policies, including public aid in case of bail-out, would create a new problem that moves internally to the protected entity with effects similar to those of the statutory mechanism of the "poison pill," that is, discouraging both internal and external parts to improve the organizational structure of the entity in question, thus causing a

f) Weak internal controls: The risk control and monitoring offices internal to financial institutions have proved ineffective both in preventing these institutions from assuming excessive levels of risk and in mitigating the risks assumed by these institutions. The remuneration policies of the managers of the financial institutions, in some cases, created an additional incentive to take on excessive risks[197].

g) Over-the-counter derivatives market: The exponential growth of the over-the-counter derivatives market, the opacity of some of the financial instruments in question, the substantial absence of regulation of the over-the-counter derivatives market and the limited use of centralized clearing houses helped to create a complex intertwining of financial relationships which made it particularly difficult to predict the effects of a bank's insolvency on the market and to intervene to prevent systemic crises.

h) Inadequate regulation of rating agencies and auditing firms: Rating agencies played a negative role in the financial crisis of 2007-2008 because they did not identify (or, at least, did not adequately identify) the risks of the complex financial products subject to their examination. They issued flattering judgments and evaluations on the basis of fallacious

---

"corporate degradation." ROE M., *Structural Corporate Degradation Due to Too-Big-to-Fail Finance*, in *University of Pennsylvania Law Review*, vol. 162, 2014, pp.1419-1464.

197 In the United States, especially following the corporate governance scandals that have emerged since 2001, the doctrine has suggested that certain remuneration practices may create "perverse" incentives, prompting managers to take excessive risks. On this point, see the analyzes and studies conducted by Lucian Bebchuk and Jesse Fried, the main spokespersons for this criticism: BEBCHUK L. A. & FRIED J. M., *Executive Compensation as an Agency Problem*, in *Journal of Economic Perspectives*, vol. 17, n. 3, 2003, pp.71-92. BEBCHUK L. A. & FRIED J. M., *Executive Compensation at Fannie Mae: A Case Study of Perverse Incentives, Nonperformance Pay, and Camouflage*, in *Journal of Corporation Law*, vol. 30, n. 4, 2005, pp.807- 822. BEBCHUK L. A. & FRIED J. M., *Pay without Performance: Overview of the Issues*, in *Journal of Corporation Law*, vol. 30, n.4, 2005, pp.647-673. In particular, it has been noted with reference to the remuneration practices of financial institutions (including banks) such as the so-called bonus guarantees according to which the bonus of an administrator would be subject to an increase in a positive scenario but not subject to a reduction in a negative scenario, they give rise to "perverse" incentives to take excessive risks. See: BEBCHUK L. A., *Bonus Guarantees can Fuel Risky Moves*, in *Wall Street Journal*, 27 August 2009, according to which: "Guaranteed bonuses create perverse incentives to take excessive risks, and they consequently could well be worse for incentives than straight salary."

evaluation models because they were based on unreasonable hypotheses or disconnected from reality. It has been observed that part of the problem could lie in the concentration of rating agencies in the market and in their conflicts of interest (the rating agencies issue judgments against the payment of commissions by the issuer of the instruments being assessed, this could undermine the objectivity of judgment by the rating agencies)[198].

It is in the context outlined above that the G20 leaders, who met in London in April 2009, concluded that the global dimensions of the crisis required a worldwide response and formally committed to do what was necessary to, among other things, strengthen the financial sector regulation would help restore market confidence[199]. Specifically, the leaders of the G20 acknowledged that the significant failures of the regulation and supervision of the financial sector were among the main causes of the crisis of 2007-2003[200]. The need to ensure greater consistency between the regulatory frameworks of the sector and financial and greater international cooperation between countries was also recognized[201]. The main objectives of the G20 leaders for strengthening the regulation and supervision of the financial sector were: (i) Promoting fairness, integrity and transparency in the market; (ii) protect against risks in the financial

---

198 HUNT J. P., *Credit Rating Agencies and the 'Worldwide Credit Crisis': The Limits of Reputation, the Insufficiency of Reform, and a Proposal for Improvement*, in *Columbia Business Law Review*, vol. 1, n. 1, 2009, p.113.

199 G20 LONDON SUMMIT, *Official Communique issued at the close of the G20 London Summit*, 2 April 2009, par. 2-4, eu-un.europa.eu/articles/en/article_8622_en.htm.

200 G20 LONDON SUMMIT, *Official Communique issued at the close of the G20 London Summit*, op.cit., par. 13 according to which: "Major failures in the financial sector and in financial regulation and supervision were fundamental causes of the crisis. Confidence will not be restored until we rebuild trust in our financial system. We will take action to build a stronger, more globally consistent, supervisory and regulatory framework for the future financial sector, which will support sustainable global growth and serve the needs of business and citizens."

201 G20 LONDON SUMMIT, *Official Communique issued at the close of the G20 London Summit*, op.cit. par. 14, according to which: "We each agree to ensure our domestic regulatory systems are strong. But we also agree to establish the much greater consistency and systematic cooperation between countries, and the framework of internationally agreed high standards, that a global financial system requires."

system; (iii) reduce the use of sources of financing whose risk is inappropriate; and (iv) to discourage excessive risk-taking[202].

The next paragraphs will illustrate the regulatory responses of the United States and the European Union to the 2007-2008 crisis, limited to the most important regulatory provisions for the private equity sector[203].

2. Regulatory framework of private equity in the United States

The United States did not delay in implementing the international agreements reached during the G20 summit held in London in the spring of 2009. On 19 June 2009 the President of the United States, Barack Obama, presented the guidelines for a radical regulatory reform of the U.S. financial sector[204]. With particular reference to the private equity industry, the Obama administration's proposal provided that investment advisers (including managers of private equity funds) were subject to registration with the U.S. Securities and Exchange Commission (hereinafter

---

202 G20 LONDON SUMMIT, *Official Communique issued at the close of the G20 London Summit*, op.cit. par. 14, according to which: "Strengthened regulation and supervision must promote propriety, integrity and transparency; guard against risk across the financial system; dampen rather than amplify the financial and economic cycle; reduce reliance on inappropriately risky sources of financing; and discourage excessive risk-taking."

203 Incidentally, the works of Roberta Romano on the limits of the regulatory reforms of the US financial sector and on legislative techniques aimed at mitigating these limits should be noted. The author notes that regulatory reforms in the US financial sector: (i) Are invariably adopted in response to financial crises, at times when there is little useful information available; (ii) prove unsuitable to face the problems that were intended to be solved; and (iii) they are difficult to modify even in cases where there seems to be political consensus; the author suggests two legislative techniques aimed at mitigating the above limits: Providing for the verification of the effectiveness and revision of the legislation after some time and mechanisms for implementing the flexible rules or subject to an initial trial period. See: ROMANO R., *Regulating in the Dark*, in *Yale Law & Economics Research Paper*, n. 442, 2012. ROMANO R., *Further Assessment of the Iron Law of Financial Regulation: A Postscript to Regulating in the Dark*, in *Yale Law & Economics Research Paper*, n. 515, 2014.

204 U.S. DEPARTMENT OF TREASURY, *Financial Regulatory Reform – A new foundation: rebuilding financial supervision and regulation*, 2009, http://www.treasury.gov/initiatives/Documents/FinalReport_web.pdf.WSJ STAFF, *Obama's Financial Reform Plan: The Condensed Version*, in *The Wall Street Journal*, 17 June 2009, http://blogs.wsj.com/washwire/2009/06/17/obamas-financial-reform-plan-the-condensed-version/.

"SEC")[205], so that the SEC could supervise them and, if necessary, intervene for the stability of the financial markets[206].

At the end of 2009, the Democratic MP Barney Frank followed the guidelines put forward by President Obama by presenting a draft regulatory measure later integrated with the proposal by Democratic Senator Chris Dodd. After various shuttles between U.S. House of Representatives and U.S. Senate, the draft measure called "Dodd-Frank Wall Street Reform and Consumer Protection Act of 2010" (hereinafter, "Dodd-Frank Act") was approved and promulgated by President Barack Obama on 21 July 2010[207].

The Dodd-Frank Act entered into force in March 2012 and represents a significant change in the US legal system because, with it, subjects (including managers of private equity and hedge funds) who had previously been able to operate independently negotiation with their counterparties and, above all, without supervision by supervisory authorities, they were subject to the control of the SEC and to a strict regulatory regime (including documentary burdens and disclosure obligations, as illustrated below).

The rationale of the Dodd-Frank Act is mainly to promote the financial stability of the United States by intervening on the liability regime and transparency of the financial sector, mitigate the problem of "too big to fail" and avoid further public interventions (therefore borne by the taxpayers) in rescue of the private financial system.

---

205 U.S. Securities and Exchange Commission (SEC) is an independent, United States federal agency with responsibility, among other things, for oversight and regulation in the US financial sector. The SEC's mission is to protect investors, to maintain fair, efficient and orderly markets, as well as to facilitate capital formation. For further information see: http://www.sec.gov/about/whatwedo.shtml#.VImPF6ahDxg

206 U.S. DEPARTMENT OF TREASURY, *Financial Regulatory Reform – A new foundation: rebuilding financial supervision and regulation*, op. cit., p. 12; WSJ STAFF, *Obama's Financial Reform Plan: The Condensed Version*, in *The Wall Street Journal*, op. cit., p.1.

207 Dodd-Frank Wall Street Reform and Consumer Protection Act of 2010, U.S. Public Law n. 111-203, 124 Stat. 1376 (2010).

The Dodd-Frank Act is a particularly voluminous measure[208] but for private equity operators it mainly notes Title IV[209] which: (i) Modifies the registration regime pursuant to the Investment Advisers Act of 1940 (hereinafter, the "advisers act")[210]; (ii) specifies the SEC's powers over investment advisers; and (iii) introduces new organizational obligations for investment advisers, including private equity operators. To understand the scope of the reform introduced by the Dodd-Frank Act, it is necessary to put this reform law in place with the provisions of the Advisers Act, as illustrated below.

The Advisers Act, as amended by the Dodd-Frank Act, concerns the regulation of the activities of investment advisers, a term defined and interpreted extensively, so as to include every subject (be it a natural or legal person) who, for consideration, provides advice, prepare reports or perform analyzes on financial instruments or investments[211]. Specifically, the Advisers Act requires investment advisers who manage assets of not less than $ 100 million and which do not fall under one of the exceptions provided therein to register with the SEC and to comply with the special regime for investment advisers subject to registration (registered investment advisers; hereinafter "RIA").

---

208 The Dodd-Frank Act has 848 pages against 29 pages of the 1864 federal law that established the US banking system, 32 pages of the 1913 Federal Reserve Act and 37 pages of the Glass-Steagall Act which represents the latest significant reform of the U.S. financial system before the Dodd-Frank Act. See: THE ECONOMIST, *Too big not to fail*, in *The Economist*, 18 February 2012, http://www.economist.com/node/21547784.

209 Title IV of the Dodd-Frank Act is entitled "Regulation of Advisers to Hedge Funds and Others."

210 15U.S.C. §80b-1 up to §80b-21. The Advisers Act is the main regulatory source in the United States system regarding investment advisers, i.e. subjects who provide consultancy services for consideration with reference to investments and financial instruments (defined and interpreted extensively).

211 CHERTOK S., *A comprehensive guide to Title IV of the Dodd-Frank Act and the rules promulgated thereunder*, in *UC Davis Business Law Journal*, vol. 12, 2012, p.130. Pursuant to the Advisers Act, §202(a)(11): ""Investment adviser" means any person who, for compensation, engages in the business of advising others, either directly or through publications or writings, as to the value of securities or as to the advisability of investing in, purchasing, or selling securities, or who, for compensation and as part of a regular business, issues or promulgates analyses or reports concerning securities."

Many of the private equity firms, as well as the general partners and advisory companies of private equity funds are therefore subject to the regime for RIAs unless one of the following exceptions is applied[212]: 1. "Private fund advisers" are excluded from the regulatory regime for RIAs under the Advisers Act, investment advisers who act exclusively on behalf of private funds and who have assets under management in the United States of less than $ 150 million[213]; 2. "foreign private fund advisers" in general, the regulatory regime for RIAs under the Advisers Act applies to non-US investment advisers limited to their dealings with US clients. 245 specifically, investment advisers are excluded from the regulatory regime for RIAs that: (a) Are not based in the United States; (b) in the previous twelve months have (i) had fewer than fifteen private fund investors and/or clients in the United States for whom they have acted as investment advisers and (ii) assets under management attributable to such investors and clients in the States United overall less than $25 million; and (c) do not present themselves to the public in the United States as investment advisers or act as investment advisers for certain investment companies[214];3."Venture capital fund advisers" are excluded from the regulatory regime for RIAs under the Advisers Act, investment advisers who act exclusively on behalf of venture capital funds[215]; 4. "SBIC investment advisers" are excluded from the regulatory regime envisaged for RIAs pursuant to the Advisers Act, investment advisers who act exclusively on behalf small business investment companies (SBIC)[216].

The regime envisaged for RIAs pursuant to the Advisers Act can be summarized in the following elements: (i) Organizational requirements, relating to the storage, maintenance and updating of certain company books, accounting records, correspondence, communications and

---

212 For the sake of completeness, it is noted that the vehicles for managing family assets (family offices) are expressly excluded from the subjective scope of application of the Advisers Act pursuant to the Dodd-Frank Act, §409 and the Advisers Act, §202 (a) (11) (G).

213 Advisers Act, §203(m)(1).

214 Advisers Act, §203(b)(3) e §202(a)(30).

215 Advisers Act, §203 (l). The term "venture capital funds" is defined in the Advisers Act through reference to secondary legislation issued by the SEC. See: SEC Release n. IA-3222, File n. S7-37- 10, U.S. Code of Federal Regulations, title 17, part 275.

216 Advisers Act, §203(b)(7).

contracts with its customers/investors, to the adoption of specific compliance policies and procedures; (ii) disclosure obligations to the SEC and the public; (iii) custody obligations for clients/investors' assets; (iv) compliance with certain mandatory rules relating to the content of contracts with customers/investors; (v) special advertising arrangements; (vi) compliance with anti-avoidance rules; and (vii) compliance with state regulations.

Finally, without prejudice to the exceptions to the registration obligation, investment advisers who rely on the exceptions for private fund advisers and venture capital funds advisers are, in any case, subject to some simplified disclosure obligations and to compliance with some general rules of a anti elusive character[217].

Under the Advisers Act, as amended by the Dodd-Frank Act, RIAs are subject to detailed organizational requirements. Specifically, RIAs are required to register, update and keep copies, among other things, of the following documents and information with reference to each entity to which they provide their services: (i) Supplementary or ancillary agreements of framework contracts in which they are envisaged more favorable conditions for one or more customers/investors; (ii) payment, investment, divestment or other related transactions; (iii) amount of assets under management, indicating the possible use of third-party loans, including off-balance sheet obligations; (iv) exposure to credit risks of contractual counterparties; (v) investment policies and procedures; (vi) investment valuation policies and procedures; (vii) type of assets that make up the assets; and (viii) any other information that may be deemed appropriate and necessary, in the public interest, by the SEC or other authority for the protection of investors from systemic risks[218].

The RIAs must also keep the company books and accounting records up to date, as well as keep copies of the communications and contracts with the subjects to whom they provide their services, in each case so that these documents and information are readily available in the

217 U.S. Code of Federal Regulations, title 17, §275.204-4(a).

218 Advisers Act, §204(b)(3); Dodd-Frank Act, §404; U.S. Code of Federal Regulations, title 17, §275.204-2.

event of a request or inspection by SEC[219]. These archiving, maintenance and updating obligations also serve to support the content of the periodic communications that the RIAs must make to the SEC or to the subjects to whom they provide their services.

RIAs must have compliance policies and procedures. Specifically, RIAs must: (i) Adopt and implement written policies and procedures that can reasonably prevent violations, by RIAs and personnel supervised by them, of the rules set out in the Advisers Act and the rules issued by the SEC in implementation of the Advisers Act; (ii) periodically, but at least annually, review the adequacy and effectiveness of the policies and procedures referred to in point (i) above; and (iii) appoint a chief compliance officer for the management of the policies and procedures referred to in point (i)[220] above.

Finally, RIAs must have an ethical code (the minimum content of which is expressly identified in the implementing rules of the Advisers Act) and ensure that periodic reports are produced to be submitted to the attention and supervision of the chief compliance officer[221].

RIAs are also subject to reporting obligations to the SEC and, in some cases, to their customers/investors. In particular, the RIAs must submit the ADV Form to the SEC -the detailed content of which is defined by SEC measures- together with their application for registration as an RIA with the SEC[222]. The ADV Form is divided into four parts: (i) Part 1A contains information relating to the RIA, to the subjects who hold direct or indirect shareholdings in the RIA, to the subjects that control the RIA and to the subjects delegated by the RIA; (ii) part 1B contains information relating to the possible registration of the RIA with state authorities in the United States; (iii) part 2A contains the so-called "brochure," i.e. a document containing information relating, among other things, to the activities of the RIA, remuneration policies, commissions,

---

219 Advisers Act, §204(a). Under the Advisers Act, the SEC must conduct periodic inspections regarding the activities of the RIAs but has the right to conduct inspections at any time.

220 U.S. Code of Federal Regulations, title 17, §275.206(4)-7.

221 U.S. Code of Federal Regulations, title 17, §275.204A-1.

222 U.S. Code of Federal Regulations, title 17, §275.203-1. With the exception of motivated exceptions, due to confidentiality requirements, the information transmitted through the ADV Form is made public by the SEC.

investment strategies, risks and any conflicts of interest of the RIA; and (iv) part 2B contains the so-called "brochure supplement," i.e. a document which indicates, among other things, information relating to managers, partners, administrators and employees of RIA[223]. RIAs must periodically update (at least annually) the ADV Form[224]. In addition, RIAs must periodically transmit updated versions of the brochure and supplementary brochure to their customers/investors[225].

RIAs that manage assets of no less than $150 million are also required to provide periodic reporting (on an annual basis or, in the case of RIAs that manage significant assets, on a quarterly basis), by submitting Form PF[226] to the SEC. The content of the PF Form varies according to the size of the RIA and the type of subject to which the RIA provides its services and can include both information relating to the RIA (including information on assets under management), and information relating to each investment fund or other collective investment scheme to which the RIA offers its services (including information relating to the gross and net value of the investments, to the overall value of the positions in financial derivative instruments, to the entities that hold significant investments in the fund or collective investment scheme, to the gross and net returns, leverage, financial valuations and valuation methodologies, liquidity of investments and portfolio companies)[227].

The RIAs must also safeguard the custody of the assets of their customers/investors and ensure that an independent auditor provides customers/investors with periodic information on the consistency of these assets[228]. The independent auditor must verify by physical inspection, to be carried out at least annually, the consistency of the assets entrusted on deposit[229].

223 U.S. Code of Federal Regulations, title 17, §275.203-1.
224 U.S. Code of Federal Regulations, title 17, §275.204-1.
225 U.S. Code of Federal Regulations, title 17, §275.204-3.
226 U.S. Code of Federal Regulations, title 17, §275.204(b)-1. The information transmitted through the PF Form is treated as confidential information both by the SEC and by other authorities or administrative agencies that may have access to it.
227 U.S. Code of Federal Regulations, title 17, §275.204(b)-1.
228 Dodd-Frank Act, §411.
229 U.S. Code of Federal Regulations, title 17, §275.206(4)-2.

Although in practice it usually does not represent a problem, pursuant to §205 (a) (1) of the Advisers Act, contractual clauses that provide for the remuneration of the RIA according to the returns of its client/investor are prohibited (the usual forecasts would therefore be prohibited relating to the payment of performance fees to the general partner) unless that client/investor meets certain minimum capital requirements. It is therefore of fundamental importance for the maintenance of the economic model of a private equity fund to verify the applicability of one of the exceptions to the prohibition of remuneration of the RIA according to the returns of its client/investor pursuant to the Advisers Act[230].

Finally, there are provisions in the Advisers Act, which regulate the content of the contracts between the RIAs and their customers/investors, the advertising of the services offered by the RIAs and the elusive conduct of the standard in question.

With regard to the content of the contracts between the RIAs and their customers/investors, the transfer of consultancy contracts between the RIAs and their customers/investors is prohibited under the Advisers Act without the prior consent of the customer/investor concerned[231]. The covenant waiver by customers/investors of compliance with the provisions of the Advisers Act by the RIA[232] is also prohibited.

As for the advertising of the services offered by the RIAs, the Advisers Act provides rules regarding the type and content of messages and information of a promotional (or more specifically advertising) nature that RIAs can disclose to the public; the rationale is obviously to protect the recipients of these messages or information[233].

Finally, as regards the anti-circumvention rules, pursuant to the Advisers Act, each investment adviser (be it an RIA or not) is prohibited from: (i) Providing false or misleading information or omitting factual circumstances, in each case with reference to significant events, in communications to investors or potential investors; and (ii) perform any fraudulent, misleading or manipulative act with reference to the

230 Advisers Act, §205(b)(4).
231 Advisers Act, §205(a)(2).
232 Advisers Act, §215(a).
233 U.S. Code of Federal Regulations, title 17, §275.206(4)-1.

aforementioned investors or potential investors[234]. Furthermore, each investment adviser (be it an RIA or not) is prohibited from providing, for consideration, its services to any government agency to which this investment adviser has made a capital contribution, for a period of two years from the date of the contribution in question (so-called "pay to play" ban)[235].

Although the Advisers Act expressly provides that U.S. state regulations may not require the registration of investment advisers who are already required to register with the SEC[236], this does not exclude investment advisers who fall under one or more of the exceptions to the registration requirement. The SEC are subject to the application of state regimes and to the supervision of state authorities.

In short, the Dodd-Frank Act marked the transition in the United States from the substantial absence of regulation and supervision of private equity operators to a regulatory regime that requires them to register with the SEC (with consequent SEC supervision) and introduces organizational requirements and disclosure obligations aimed at ensuring transparency in the market, as well as the possibility for the authorities to intervene in the event of systemic risks or danger to the stability of the financial system.

The main criticism of the Dodd-Frank Act, from the point of view of private equity operators, is that the Dodd-Frank Act has also attracted the private equity sector into the regulatory framework, although the law in question aims to protect the market systemic risk finance and experts agree that private equity is not a source of systemic risk[237]. The point is, therefore, that the charges and costs imposed by the Dodd-Frank Act would not be necessary and would make the private equity market less efficient.

---

234 U.S. Code of Federal Regulations, title 17, §275.206(4)-8.
235 U.S. Code of Federal Regulations, title 17, §275.206(4)-5.
236 Advisers Act, §203A(b)(1).
237 SERETAKIS A., *A comparative examination of private equity in the United States and Europe: accounting for the past and predicting the future*, in *Fordham Journal of Corporate & Financial Law*, vol. XVIII, 2013, p.658.

3. Regulation framework of private equity in the European Union

The financial crisis of 2007-2008 highlighted, among other things, the shortcomings of the regulatory framework and the supervisory system of European financial markets and, in particular, shortcomings in transparency in the market, uniform application of EU law, cooperation and coordination between national authorities. Thus a process of analysis and reform of the regulatory framework was launched aimed at reforming the supervisory systems, strengthening the level of transparency to protect investors, restoring confidence in the market and minimizing the risk of future financial crises[238].

In the period between July 2008 and February 2009 - therefore before the G20 leaders' summit held in London in April 2009 - three reports of European experts were drawn up[239] which laid the foundations for the subsequent drafting of the first draft directive on fund managers of alternative investments (the managers, hereinafter "AIFM;" and the funds, hereinafter, "AIF"). Months of intense work followed by the various European institutions, especially by the European Commission, to define a shared text. The AIFM Directive was published in the official journal of the European Union on 1 July 2011, the provision entered into force on 21 July 2011 and the deadline for transposition by the Member States expired on 22 July 2013[240].

---

238 CONSOB, *Relazione sull'attività di Analisi di Impatto della Regolamentazione – Attuazione della Direttiva sui gestori di fondi di investimento alternativi (AIFMD)*, 2014, p.2. ZETSCHE D.A., *The AIFM Directive 2011/61/EU European Regulation of Alternative Investment Funds*, New York, USA, Kluwer Law International, 2013.

239 It is intended to refer to the following reports (1) Lehne report, dated 9 July 2008, http://www.europarl.europa.eu/sides/getDoc.do?pubRef=-//EP//TEXT+REPORT+A6-2008 0296+0+DOC+XML+V0//EN. (2)Rasmussen report, dated 11 September 2008, http:// www.europarl.europa.eu / sides/getDoc.do?pubRef=-// EP//TEXT+REPORT+ A6-2008- 0338+0+DOC+XML+V0//EN&language=en, and (3) De Larosière report, of 25 February 2009, http://ec.europa.eu/internal_market/finances/docs/de_larosiere _report_en.pdf.

240 The directive is, in fact, a regulatory act addressed to Member States which, pursuant to art. 288 (3) of the Treaty on the Functioning of the European Union, "binds the Member State to which it is addressed as regards the result to be achieved, without prejudice to the competence of the national bodies with regard to form and means." It should be noted that the deadline by which the European directive must be transposed is relevant, among other things, for the purposes of the applicability of the principle of

The objectives of the AIFM Directive, as identified by the European Commission, are: (i) To increase the level of transparency of AIFMs towards investors, supervisors and employees of portfolio companies; (ii) to equip national and European authorities with the information and tools necessary to monitor and respond to the risk of stability of the financial system that may be caused or amplified by the activity of AIFMs; (iii) introduce a common and solid approach towards investor protection in AIFs; (iv) strengthen and expand the single market, creating the conditions for a wider choice by investors and greater competition within the European Union on the basis of a strong and uniform regulatory framework; and (v) increase the level of liability of AIFMs who gain control of unlisted companies towards the employees of those companies and the market in general[241]. Specifically, with reference to strengthening supervision, the objective is to implement a "double track of "macro-prudential supervision," aimed at controlling and assessing the risks to financial stability deriving from macroeconomic and financial system developments as a whole and of "micro-prudential supervision," aimed at safeguarding the stability of market participants and protecting investors"[242].

The AIFM Directive was followed by transposition acts at national level by the Member States of the European Union, delegated

"direct effect" of the directive, i.e. the attribution of rights to individuals, in the case of the obligations in this directive they are precise, clear and unconditional and do not require complementary national or European measures. For further information on the direct effectiveness of EU directives, see: CRAIG P. & DE BÚRCA G., *EU Law – Text, Cases, and Materials*, Oxford, UK, Oxford University Press, 2011, p.180 ss.

241 EUROPEAN COMMISSION, *Press release – Directive on Alternative Investment Fund Managers ('AIFMD'): Frequently Asked Questions*, Memo/10/572, 2011.

242 CONSOB, *Relazione sull'attività di Analisi di Impatto della Regolamentazione – Attuazione della Direttiva sui gestori di fondi di investimento alternativi (AIFMD)*, op.cit., p.3.

acts[243], implementing measures[244], as well as -particularly relevant for the purposes of this work- the guidelines of the European Securities and Markets Authority (ESMA) which is the main European authority responsible for supervising the AIFM[245].

The provisions of greatest interest to private equity operators introduced by the AIFM Directive will be briefly illustrated below and concern: (i) The organizational requirements, in particular the requirements of minimum capitalization, risk management and liquidity management; (ii) disclosure obligations; (iii) the custody obligations of the AIF's assets; (iv) the remuneration policies of the AIFM; and (v) the anti-unbundling provisions of the activities.

Hence, the AIFM Directive contains rules on the authorization, operation and transparency of alternative investment fund managers (AIFMs) that manage and/or market alternative investment funds (AIFs) -including private equity funds- in the European Union[246].

Specifically, the directive in question applies to: (i) AIFMs having their registered office in one of the Member States (hereinafter, "EU AIFM"); (ii) AIFMs which do not have their registered office in one of the Member States of the European Union (hereinafter, "non-EU AIFM") but which manage one or more AIFs authorized, registered or having their registered office in one of the Member States of the European Union (hereafter, "AIF EU"); and (iii) non-EU AIFMs that market one or more

---

243 In particular, it refers to: (i) Delegated regulation (EU) n. 231/2013 of the Commission of 19 December 2012 which integrates Directive 2011/61/EU of the European Parliament and of the Council as regards general operating exemptions, custodians, financial leverage, transparency and surveillance; and (ii) delegated regulation (EU) n. 694/2014 of the Commission of 17 December 2013 which integrates Directive 2011/61/EU of the European Parliament and of the Council as regards the regulatory technical standards that establish the types of managers of alternative investment funds.

244 In particular, it refers to: (i) Implementing Regulation (EU) n. 447/2013 of the Commission of 15 May 2013 which establishes the procedure applicable to AIFMs that choose to submit to the rules of Directive 2011/61/EU of the European Parliament and of the Council; and (ii) implementing regulation (EU) n. 448/2013 of the Commission of 15 May 2013 which establishes the procedure for determining the reference Member State of the non-EU AIFM pursuant to Directive 2011/61/EU of the European Parliament and of the Council.

245 In particular, it refers to the ESMA/2013/232 Guidelines for sound remuneration policies pursuant to the AIFM Directive of 1 July 2013.

246 AIFM Directive (2011/61/EU), art. 1.

AIFs in the European Union (whether they are EU AIFs or not)[247]. The following are excluded from the subjective scope, among others: (i) Corporate or professional pension institutions that fall within the scope of Directive 2003/41/EC3[248]; (ii) supranational institutions (e.g. the European Investment Bank and the European Investment Fund); and (iii) AIFMs managing one or more AIFs whose only investors are the AIFMs themselves or other entities belonging to the same corporate group (e.g. captive funds)[249]. Finally, a simplified regulatory regime is envisaged for AIFMs whose assets under management are less than € 100 million (or € 500 million if the AIF does not use leverage)[250].

The main purpose of the AIFM Directive is the authorization regime: No AIFM (which falls within the subjective scope of the directive in question) can manage or market AIFs without the authorization of the competent supervisory authority but, once issued, this authorization is valid for all Member States (so-called "EU passport")[251]. The EU passport is probably the greatest opportunity offered by the AIFM Directive to private equity operators.

For clarity: The AIFM Directive does not regulate AIFs (which continue to be regulated at national level) but only AIFMs, i.e. the managers of such AIFs[252].

AIFMs must also comply with specific capital and organizational requirements. Specifically, AIFMs must have an initial capital of at least € 125,000, or € 300,000 if the AIFMs are AIFs managed internally (for example in the case of fixed capital investment companies)[253] and an additional amount equal to 0,02% of the amount for which the value of the AIFM's portfolios exceeds €250,000,000. The total of the initial capital and additional amount cannot exceed €10,000,000[254]. In order to deal with

247 AIFM Directive (2011/61/EU), art. 2 (1).
248 Directive 2003/41/EC of the European Parliament and of the Council of 3 June 2003 relating to the activities and supervision of corporate or professional pension institutions.
249 AIFM Directive (2011/61/EU), articles 2 (3) and 3 (1).
250 AIFM Directive (2011/61/EU), art. 3.
251 AIFM Directive (2011/61/EU), articles 6 and 8 (1).
252 AIFM Directive (2011/61/EU), premise (10).
253 Legislative Decree of 24 February 1998, n. 58, part II, title III, Chapter I-bis, section II.
254 AIFM Directive (2011/61/EU), art. 9 (1)-9(3).

potential professional liability risks arising from the activities that AIFMs may carry out, AIFMs must have additional and adequate own funds to cover potential risks arising from professional negligence or hold a professional negligence liability insurance policy that is adequate to the risks covered. The European implementing legislation specifies that, with exceptions, the amount of additional own funds must be at least equal to 0.01% of the value of the portfolios of the managed AIFs, while insurance coverage must be at least equal to 0.9% of the value of the portfolios of the AIFs managed[255].

As for the internal organization, pursuant to the directive in question, AIFMs must at all times resort to adequate human and technical resources for the good management of AIFs[256]. AIFMs must also have: (i) A good administrative and accounting organization; (ii) control and safeguard methods for electronic data processing; and (iii) adequate internal control procedures which include, in particular, rules for the personal operations of employees or for the holding or management of investments for investment purposes on their own account and which ensure, at the very least, that any transaction in which the AIF intervenes, can be recognized as regards the origin, the parts, the nature and the place and the moment in which it was carried out and that the activities of the AIF managed by the AIFM are invested in accordance with the regulation or its constitutive documents and the current regulatory provisions. The European implementing legislation, among other things, specifies the general principles relating to the organizational requirements[257], the characteristics of the aforementioned electronic data processing systems[258], the accounting policies and procedures to ensure the protection of investors[259], the criteria for the internal distribution of the control functions[260], the characteristics of the permanent conformity control functions[261] and internal audit[262], the procedures and provisions aimed at

---

255 Delegated Regulation (EU) n. 231/2013, articles 14 (2) and 15 (4).
256 AIFM Directive (2011/61/EU), art. 18 (1).
257 Delegated Regulation (EU) n. 231/2013, art. 57.
258 Delegated Regulation (EU) n. 231/2013, art. 58.
259 Delegated Regulation (EU) n. 231/2013, art. 59.
260 Delegated Regulation (EU) n. 231/2013, art. 60.
261 Delegated Regulation (EU) n. 231/2013, art. 61.
262 Delegated Regulation (EU) n. 231/2013, art. 62.

avoiding and managing conflicts of interest[263] and the procedures and obligations regarding the recording and conservation of operations[264].

As regards risk management, AIFMs must separate, both functionally and hierarchically, the risk management functions from the operating units (including the investment portfolio management functions)[265]. The European implementing legislation, among other things, specifies the minimum structural and organizational requirements of the risk management function of AIFMs[266], the minimum content of risk management policies[267], the assessment, surveillance and periodic review of management systems risk, the criteria and procedures for measuring and managing risk[268], and the minimum procedures and guarantees against conflicts of interest[269]. With reference to leverage, AIFMs must set, on the basis of criteria identified in the AIFM Directive, the maximum level of leverage to be used on behalf of each AIF they manage[270].

The AIFM Directive also requires that AIFMs that manage AIFs other than closed-end funds have an adequate liquidity management system and adopt procedures that allow them to control the liquidity risk of the AIF and ensure that the liquidity profile of the investments of the FIA complies with the underlying obligations. AIFMs must also regularly carry out stress tests, under normal and exceptional liquidity conditions, which allow them to assess the liquidity risk of the AIFs and consequently to control the liquidity risk of the AIFs[271].

The AIFM Directive and the European implementing legislation provide for detailed reporting obligations on AIFMs which can be divided into four categories: 1.Information to investors prior to investment in AIFs - for each of the EU AIFs they manage and for each of the AIFs they manage- market in the European Union, AIFMs make available to investors in the AIF, in accordance with the regulation or the constituent

---

263 Delegated Regulation (EU) n. 231/2013, art. 63.
264 Delegated Regulation (EU) n. 231/2013, art. 64-66.
265 AIFM Directive (2011/61/EU), art. 18 (1).
266 Delegated Regulation (EU) n. 231/2013, art. 38-39.
267 Delegated Regulation (EU) n. 231/2013, art. 40.
268 Delegated Regulation (EU) n. 231/2013, art. 45.
269 Delegated Regulation (EU) n. 231/2013, art. 43.
270 AIFM Directive (2011/61/EU), art. 15 (4).
271 AIFM Directive (2011/61/EU), art. 16 (1).

documents of the AIF, among other things, the following information: (i) A description of the AIF's investment strategy and objectives, the types of assets in which the fund may invest, the techniques it can use and all associated risks, as well as the maximum level of leverage that the AIFM is authorized to use on behalf of the AIF; (ii) a description of the procedures according to which the AIF can change its investment strategy or investment policy; (iii) a description of the main legal implications of the contractual relationship established for the purposes of the investment; (iv) the identity of the AIFM, the depository of the AIF, the auditor and any other service provider, as well as a description of their duties and investor rights; (v) a description of how the AIFM meets the coverage requirement for potential professional liability risks; (vi) a description of any delegated management function; (vii) a description of the procedure and methodology for evaluating the AIF's assets; (viii) a description of the AIF's liquidity risk management; (ix) a description of all commissions, costs and expenses and their maximum amounts, directly or indirectly borne by investors; and (x) a description of any preferential treatment reserved for some investors[272].

2.Periodic information to AIF investors. The AIFM is required, for each EU AIF that manages and for each AIF that markets in the European Union, to make available to investors and supervisors an annual report which includes, among the others, the following elements: (i) The AIF's balance sheet and balance sheet; (ii) the income and expenses account for the year; (iii) a report on the activities carried out during the year; and (iv) the total remuneration amounts for the year, divided into fixed and variable remuneration, paid by the AIFM to its staff and the number of beneficiaries as well as, if applicable, the performance fee paid by the AIF[273].

3.Reporting to supervisors. AIFMs regularly provide national supervisors with information on the main financial instruments they trade, the markets in which they are members or where they actively trade and the main exposures and the most important concentrations of each AIF they manage. Among other information, they provide the following: (i)

---

272 AIFM Directive (2011/61/EU), art. 23.
273 AIFM Directive (2011/61/EU), art. 22.

The percentage of AIF assets subject to special provisions due to their illiquid nature; (ii) any new measures adopted to manage the liquidity of the AIF; (iii) the risk profile of the AIF and the risk management systems used by the AIFM to manage market risk, liquidity risk, counterparty risk and other risks, including operational risk; (iv) information on the main categories of assets in which the AIF has invested; and (v) the results of stress tests performed in accordance with the AIFM Directive. For the sake of completeness, it should be noted that AIFMs are subject to cooperation obligations with supervisory authorities for the monitoring of systemic risk as well as to ensure the stability and integrity of the financial system[274].

4.Special communications in the case of the purchase of significant holdings in portfolio companies. If an AIF holds or disposes of shares in an unlisted company, the AIFM managing this AIF shall notify the competent authorities in its member state of the proportion of the company's voting rights not listed in the possession of the AIF every time this percentage reaches, exceeds or falls below certain thresholds[275]. Furthermore, if an AIF acquires control, individually or jointly, of an unlisted company, the AIFMs managing this AIF communicate the acquisition of control and some additional information (briefly illustrated below) to the company being acquired and to the shareholders of such companies and ensure that the board of directors of the company being acquired extends the communication to the workers' representatives (or, in the absence of representatives, to the workers themselves)[276]. AIFMs must also communicate their intentions to workers in relation to the future activity of the unlisted company being acquired and the likely repercussions on employment, including any significant change in working conditions[277]. The AIFMs also provide annual updates in which they describe, among other things, the foreseeable evolution of the company being acquired[278].

274 AIFM Directive (2011/61/EU), art. 22.
275 AIFM Directive (2011/61/EU), art. 27 (1).
276 AIFM Directive (2011/61/EU), artt. 27-28.
277 AIFM Directive (2011/61/EU), art. 28(4).
278 AIFM Directive (2011/61/EU), art. 29(2).

In order to avoid the repetition of scandals similar to the financial fraud perpetrated by Bernard Madoff[279], the European legislator has deemed it appropriate to separate the custody of assets from management functions and to distinguish the assets of investors from that of the manager. The AIFM Directive expressly indicates that although AIFMs manage AIFs according to different business models and methods, for example for the custody of assets, it is essential that a depositary other than the AIFM is designated to exercise the depositary functions with respect to the AIF[280]. The AIFM[281] Directive and the European implementing legislation[282] specify the subjective and objective requirements of the depositary, as well as the minimum elements that must be expressly provided for in the contract with the depositary and the regime of liability of the depositary towards the AIF and the investors.

The premises of the AIFM Directive indicate that in order to counter the potentially negative effects of poorly conceived remuneration regimes on the healthy management of risks and on the control of risk taking by individuals, it is necessary to provide for the explicit obligation on AIFMs to create and maintain for the categories of subjects whose professional activity has a significant impact on the risk profiles of the AIFs they manage, remunerative policies and practices in line with healthy and effective risk management[283]. These categories of individuals should include at least senior managers, individuals who take on risk, staff who

---

279 Bernard (Bernie) Madoff - arrested in late 2008 and sentenced to 150 years in prison for fraud and other crimes that caused damage and financial shortages of over $50 billion- presented himself to individuals with high capital availability as a skilled investment manager in able to ensure minimum returns of 10% -12% per annum on the capital entrusted to it in management. In reality the capitals were opportunistically distracted in favor of Madoff himself who for over twenty years managed to deceive his investors by repaying, when required, the portions of capital and interest thanks to the financial funding created through new capital injections entrusted to him in management. The fraudulent scheme was discovered when, following the 2007-2008 crisis, Madoff was unable to honor multiple requests for divestment and repayment of capital due to the lack of available financial resources. For further information see: THE ECONOMIST, *The Madoff Affair – Con of the century*, in *The Economist*, 18 December 2008, http://www.economist.com/node/12818310

280 AIFM Directive (2011/61/EU), premise (32).

281 AIFM Directive (2011/61/EU), art. 21.

282 Delegated Regulation (EU) n. 231/2013, art. 83.

283 AIFM Directive (2011/61/EU), premise (24).

perform control functions and any employee who receives an overall remuneration who places him in the same remuneration bracket as senior management and those who take on the risk.

Specifically, Annex II of the AIFM Directive provides that: "In developing and applying the overall remuneration policies, which include discretionary remuneration and pension benefits, for the categories of personnel including senior managers, the persons who hire the risk, the personnel who perform control functions and any employee who receives an overall remuneration who places it in the same remuneration bracket as senior management and those who assume the risk, whose professional activities have a significant impact on the risk profiles of the AIFMs or the AIFs they manage, AIFMs, in the manner and appropriate to their size, internal organization and the nature, extent and complexity of their activities, adhere to the following principles: (a) The remuneration policy reflects and promotes sound and effective risk management and does not encourage taking risks that is not consistent with the risk profiles, regulations or constituent documents of the AIFs they manage; (b) the remuneration policy is in line with the business strategy, objectives, values and interests of the AIFM and the AIFs that it manages or of the investors of these funds and includes measures aimed at avoiding conflicts of interest; (c) the management body of the AIFM adopts, in its supervisory function, and periodically reviews the general principles of the remuneration policy and is responsible for its implementation; (d) the implementation of the remuneration policy is subject, at least annually, to a central and independent internal review, aimed at verifying compliance with the remuneration policies and procedures adopted by the administrative body in its supervisory function; (e) staff members engaged in control functions are remunerated in accordance with the achievement of the objectives related to their functions, regardless of the results achieved by the areas of the company subject to their supervision; (f) the remuneration of the senior managers of the risk control and compliance functions is directly controlled by the remuneration committee; (g) when the remuneration is linked to the results, the total amount of the remuneration is based on a combination of evaluations of the results of the individual and of the business unit concerned or of the AIF concerned and of the general results of the AIFM, and in the evaluation of the results individual are considered financial and non-financial criteria; (h) the evaluation of the results is performed within a multi-year framework appropriate to the life cycle of the AIF managed by the AIFM, so as to ensure that the evaluation process is based on longer-term results and that the effective payment of the remuneration components based on the results, spread over a period that takes into account the repayment policy of the AIF that it manages and the investment risks associated with it; (i) the guaranteed variable remuneration is exceptional, it is granted only if new staff are hired and limited to the first year; (j) the fixed and variable components of the overall remuneration are adequately balanced and the fixed component represents a sufficiently high part of the overall remuneration to allow the implementation of a fully flexible policy on variable components, including the possibility of not paying the variable component of remuneration; (k) the payments relating to the early termination of the contract reflect the results provided over time and are designed in such a way as not to reward the failures; (l) the measurement of results, used as a basis for calculating the variable components of individual or collective remuneration, provides for a complete adjustment aimed at integrating all the relevant types of present and future risks; (m) depending on the legal structure of the AIF and its regulations or constituent documents, a substantial part, but in any case at least 50% of any variable remuneration, is made up of units or shares of the AIF concerned, equity investments equivalent, equity-related instruments or other equivalent non-monetary instruments, unless the management of the AIF represents less than 50% of the total portfolio managed by the AIFM, in which case the minimum of 50% does not apply; […] (n) a substantial part, and in any case at least 40%, of the variable component of the remuneration, is deferred over an appropriate period in consideration of the life cycle and repayment policy of the AIF concerned and is correctly aligned with the type of risks of the AIF concerned. The period referred to in this letter is at least three to five years unless the life cycle of the AIF concerned is shorter; the remuneration payable according to deferral mechanisms is attributed no faster than pro rata; if the variable component of the remuneration represents a particularly high amount, at least 60% of this amount is deferred; (o) variable remuneration, including the deferred part, is paid or attributed only if it is sustainable with respect to the financial situation of the AIFM as a whole and justified in the light of the results of the business unit, the AIF and the person concerned. The overall variable remuneration is generally reduced considerably if the results of the AIFM or of the AIF concerned are lower than expected or negative, taking into account both the current incentives and the reductions in payments of amounts previously acquired, also through malus or restitution arrangements; (p) the pension policy is in line with the corporate strategy, objectives, values and long-term interests of the AIFM and the AIFs it manages. If the employee leaves the AIFM before retirement, discretionary pension rights are retained by the AIFM for a period of five years in the form of the instruments referred to in point (m). In the event that an employee retires, discretionary pension benefits are paid to the employee in the form of instruments referred to in letter (m), subject to a five-year maintenance period; (q) staff are required not to use personal hedging strategies or remuneration and liability insurance policies designed to affect the risk alignment effects inherent in their remuneration mechanisms; (r) variable remuneration is not paid through tools or in ways that facilitate the circumvention of the provisions of this directive"[284].

The provisions of the AIFM Directive and ESMA guidelines issued in its implementations[285] therefore have a direct impact not only on the remuneration policies of the private equity firm (that is, on the relationship between the private equity fund, on the one hand, and the private equity firm, on the other) but also on the remuneration policies internal to the private equity firm (that is, on the relationship between the private equity firm, on the one hand, and its employees and professionals, on the other). The aforementioned forecasts, as already indicated, seem to be able to mitigate the misalignment between the interests of the private equity firm and the interests of investors created by the current market

---

284 AIFM Directive (2011/61/EU), Annex II - Remuneration Policy. BROWN G.W., GREDIL O.R., KAPLAN S.N., *Do private equity funds manipulate reported returns?*, in *Journal of Financial Economics*, 132 (2), 2019, pp. 269ss.

285 ESMA/2013/232 guidelines for sound remuneration policies pursuant to the AIFM Directive of 1 July 2013.

terms relating to the (indirect) remuneration of the private equity firm. Specifically, the provisions of the AIFM Directive aimed at avoiding "an assumption of risks that is not congruent with the risk profiles [...] of the AIFs"[286] and that the AIFM is rewarded even in the event of failure of the AIF's investments seem consistent with the recommendation to correlate the management fees to the operating costs of the AIFM in order to avoid that the remuneration deriving from the fees in question is excessive, increasing the risk appetite of the AIFM[287]. Also the mechanisms of malus or refund of the variable remuneration referred to in AIFM Directive seem consistent with the recommendation to structure the performance fees according to the "European modality" precisely in order to avoid that the AIFM has interests misaligned with respect to the interests of its investors for as regards the timing of the divestments or the volatility of the investment portfolio of the AIF[288]. Finally, the measures referred to in the AIFM Directive aimed at avoiding conflicts of interest seem consistent with the recommendation to abolish lump-sum commissions for corporate transactions (transaction fees) as a harbinger of a potential conflict of interest between the AIFM that would have an interest in engaging portfolio companies. in corporate transactions in order to collect the commissions in question and the portfolio companies (therefore, indirectly, the AIF and the investors in the AIF)[289].

To protect portfolio companies, the directive in question provides that AIFMs whose AIFs acquire control of a company (listed or not), for a period of twenty-four months from the purchase of control over the company: (i) They must not facilitate, to support or order any distribution, reduction of capital, redemption of shares and/or purchase of treasury shares by this company; (ii) to the extent that they are authorized to vote on behalf of their AIFs within the governing bodies of that company, they must not vote in favor of a distribution, a capital reduction, a redemption of shares and/or a purchase of treasury shares by this company; and (iii) must in any case do everything in their power to avoid distributions, capital

286AIFM Directive (2011/61/EU), Annex II - Remuneration Policy, art. 1 (a).
287AIFM Directive (2011/61/EU), Annex II - Remuneration Policy, art. 1 (k).
288AIFM Directive (2011/61/EU), Annex II - Remuneration Policy, art. 1 (o).
289AIFM Directive (2011/61/EU), Annex II - Remuneration Policy, art. 1 (b).

reductions, redemptions of shares, and/or purchases of treasury shares by that company[290].

Finally, the AIFM Directive was criticized as a "curious and politicized legislative text"[291]. Indeed, private equity has been attracted to the regulatory area despite the intention of the legislator to regulate hedge funds[292]. Specifically, the AIFM Directive has been approved to combat systemic risks and increase transparency in the financial sector, but experts note that private equity is hardly the cause of systemic risks[293]. For this reason, the extension of the scope to the private equity industry is, at least, doubtful. A cause for concern could have been the impact of the possible bankruptcy of portfolio companies acquired from private equity funds through leveraged buy-outs (hence third party financing) on the banking industry. However, as also observed by the European Central Bank, corporate acquisitions through leveraged buy-outs do not pose a significant systemic risk for the banking sector. Moreover, even assuming that acquisitions through leveraged buy-outs posed a significant systemic risk for the banking sector, it would have been reasonable and more effective to intervene directly on this sector[294]. As regards the strict disclosure obligations envisaged by the AIFM Directive towards investors, it has been observed that these obligations do not seem necessary in consideration of the sophistication of investors in private equity funds and their ability to request and negotiate disclosure rights

---

290 AIFM Directive (2011/61/EU), premise (57) and art. 30.

291 MURRAY-JONES A., *Alternative Investment Fund Managers Directive*, in *Skadden, Arps, Slate, Meagher & Flom LLP Memo,* 29 November 2010, https://www.skadden.com/insights/alternative- investment-fund-managers-directive, according to which: "The Directive is a very odd, political piece of law making." SERETAKIS A., *A comparative examination of private equity in the United States and Europe: accounting for the past and predicting the future*, op.cit., p.658.

292 PAYNE J, *Private equity and its regulation in Europe*, in *Oxford Legal Research Paper Series*, Paper n. 40/2011,2011, p. 21, http://papers.ssrn.com/sol3/papers.cfm?abstract_id=1886186.

293 SERETAKIS A., *A comparative examination of private equity in the United States and Europe: accounting for the past and predicting the future*, op.cit., p.659.

294 SHASHA D., *The inner circle of systemic risk*, in *The Wall Street Journal*, 10 March 2009, http://blogs.wsj.com/privateequity/2009/03/10/the-inner-circle-of-systemic-risk/, which reports the words of Viral Acharya as follows: "The problem is not private equity funds per se. If banks were not lending so cheaply, private equity funds would not have levered up so much. You need to fix the banking sector, rather than going after private investors directly."

(which, moreover, occurred before the introduction of the AIFM Directive)[295]. The requirements relating to the investment portfolio valuation procedures and methodologies also seem relevant only for hedge funds, not also for private equity funds. The custody obligations under the AIFM Directive serve primarily to avoid new Madoff-style fraud. However, it has been observed that the nature of private equity investments (in consideration of the public nature or illiquidity of the assets) makes fraud similar to that perpetrated by Bernard Madoff practically impossible[296].

Summarizing in cost/benefit perspective, the AIFM Directive seems to offer attractive opportunities for private equity operators (for example, the possibility of operating throughout the European Union under an "EU passport" regime, harmonization of the regulatory framework within the European Union and the creation of a quality standard for AIFMs that should strengthen investor confidence) against significant charges and costs for private equity operators (for example, for the fulfillment of organizational requirements, custody of assets, information obligations, remuneration policies and adaptation of contracts). In view of the limited observation period since the entry into force of the AIFM Directive, it seems premature to draw conclusions on the net effect between costs and benefits of the AIFM Directive, but it is not at all obvious that the net effect is positive.

4. Comparative analysis of private equity regulation in the United States and the European Union

Both the Dodd-Frank Act and the AIFM Directive are driven by the same agreements reached at the international level during the G20 summit in London. Although the needs and objectives were common, the

295 SERETAKIS A., *A comparative examination of private equity in the United States and Europe: accounting for the past and predicting the future*, op.cit., p.659.
296 AWREY D., *The Limits of EU Hedge Fund Regulation*, in *Oxford Legal Studies – Research Paper*, n. 8/2011, 2011, p.19, according to which: "It is far more difficult, however, to understand the rationale for imposing these requirements on, for example, private equity funds. The long term, illiquid and typically very public nature of the investments made by these institutions virtually eliminates the potential for Madoff-type fraud."

regulatory responses of the United States and the European Union created divergent regulatory frameworks, as illustrated below.

A first point of divergence regards the capitalization charges: The European regulation - unlike the US regulation - provides for minimum capitalization charges for the private equity fund manager according to the size of the assets under management and requires the underwriting of insurance policies (or the provision of additional funds) to cover possible risks for professional liability. The two regulatory approaches are better understood and must be contextualized in light of the different positions of the US and European legal doctrine with reference to the value and function of the share capital and the protection mechanisms of third party creditors[297].

A second point of divergence concerns the organizational requirements of the private equity fund manager: Once again, European discipline - unlike the US one - appears more detailed and seems to impose more onerous organizational obligations, for example to ensure compliance with European legislation with reference to potential conflicts of interest, risk management, liquidity management and delegation of functions.

A third point of divergence concerns the charges and disclosure obligations for the private equity fund manager: Regardless of the content of the periodic disclosures to investors, European regulations - unlike the US one - provide for specific disclosure obligations for the fund manager

---

297 For an analytical discussion of the arguments offered by the doctrine see: GINEVRA E., *Oltre il capitale sociale? Spunti per la ripresa del dibattito sulla riforma della struttura finanziaria delle società di capitali*, in *La struttura finanziaria e i bilanci delle società di capitali – Studi in onore di Giovanni E. Colombo* (ed.by Aa. Vv.), Torino (Italia), Giappichelli, 2011, p.3 ss.. MACHADO F. S., *Effective Creditor Protection in Private Companies: Mandatory Minimum Capital Rules or Ex Post Mechanisms?*, Mimeo, 2010. EWANG F. N., *An Analysis and Critique of the European Union's Minimum Capitalization Requirement*, in *Charles Sturt University (Australia) Working Papers*, 2007. LUTTER E., *Legal Capital in Europe*, in *European Company and Financial Law Review*, vol. 1, 2006. ARMOUR J., *Legal Capital: an Outdated Concept?*, in *Centre for Business Research – University of Cambridge*, Working Paper n. 320, 2006. MACEY J. R. & ENRIQUES L., *Creditors Versus Capital Formation: The Case Against the European Legal Capital Rules*, in *Cornell Law Review*, vol. 86, 2000-2001, pp. 1165-1204. SPOLIDORO M. S., voce *Capitale sociale*, in *Enciclopedia del diritto*, IV aggiornamento, Milano, Italy, Giuffrè, 2000.

of private equity in the event of the purchase of control or significant investments in portfolio companies.

A fourth point of divergence concerns the remuneration policies of the private equity fund manager: The European discipline - unlike the United States discipline - provides detailed rules relating to the principles to which the remuneration policies and practices must be informed, the relationship between the fixed part and variable part of the remuneration of private equity firm professionals, the mechanisms for adjusting the remuneration in the event of negative or lower than expected returns on the fund, the extension of the forecast to employees with functions or remuneration comparable to that of the fund manager's top functions of investment. The U.S. regulation instead seems to limit itself to prohibiting the signing of agreements that provide for performance fees unless the client meets certain minimum capital requirements or falls within one of the other exceptions, otherwise leaving the discipline to the free negotiation of the parties.

A fifth point of divergence concerns the rules to protect the capital integrity of the portfolio company: European regulation - unlike the United States regulation - prohibits the execution of certain operations on the capital of portfolio companies in the twenty-four months following the purchase of control of such portfolio companies. The rule is aimed at protecting the capital integrity of portfolio companies and discouraging speculative transactions by private equity funds, but in view of the limited observation period since the entry into force of the AIFM Directive, it is still not possible to assess to what extent this rule achieves the desired objectives.

In short, both European and US legislation are the direct result of a regulatory reaction to the financial crisis of 2007-2008 but the two regulatory regimes are substantially different and it does not seem that legislators have managed to coordinate their work in order to produce a common response on a global scale (as hoped for at the G20 summit in London and as probably also private equity operators and professionals would hope for). In general, the European regime imposes new and greater burdens on operators, especially in terms of fulfilments, organizational requirements and disclosure obligations. Overall, the US regulatory framework appears more permissive and less burdensome than the European regulatory framework and this seems consistent with the deep-rooted (and consolidated) experience of private equity in the United States[298].

Taking into account the comparative analysis of regulatory frameworks in the United States and the European Union, models and prospects for development of the private equity market will be hypothesized below.

5. Development prospects and future scenarios of the private equity market

A recent survey of the chief financial officers of private equity firms worldwide shows that the main challenge for private equity firms in the coming years will be to face the new regulatory framework introduced by the Dodd-Frank Act and the AIFM Directive[299].

The comparative analysis carried out in the previous paragraph has shown that the European private equity regulation imposes higher charges than the US regulation and, according to a recent survey among private equity operators, these higher charges translate into higher compliance costs with the result that private equity fund managers operating in the European Union will be subject to higher regulatory costs[300]. Specifically, these are higher financial charges relating to costs for the support staff of the compliance functions, to fees for legal services

---

298 SERETAKIS A., *A comparative examination of private equity in the United States and Europe: accounting for the past and predicting the future*, op.cit., p.662.

299 ERNST&YOUNG & PEI, *Navigating the headwinds – 2014 global private equity survey*, New York, USA, 2014, pp.7-29. The respondents identified the main business challenges of private equity firms in this order: (i) Regulatory framework; (ii) competition for fundraising; (iii) further investor claims, for example greater transparency; (iv) investment activity; (v) platforms for account management; (vi) guidelines of the association of limited partners (ILPA); (vii) diversification of investments.

300 KPMG, AIMA & MFA, *The cost of compliance*, New York, USA, 2013, p.10, http://www.kpmg.com/dutchcaribbean/en/Documents/Publications/The-cost-of-compliance-v2.pdf. SERETAKIS A., *A comparative examination of private equity in the United States and Europe: accounting for the past and predicting the future*, op.cit., p.660.

and to fees for services provided for by the new regulatory framework (for example, the custody services of the fund's assets).

We will analyze which options the private equity firms have to allocate the higher costs imposed by the new regulatory framework. In the reference scenario it is assumed that the conditions of the private equity market remain stable (both from the point of view of the number of investment opportunities and from the point of view of investment returns), that investors in private equity funds can freely also access alternative investments to private equity investments and that private equity firms have competence levels, access to homogeneous investment opportunities and profitability, with the exception of the regulatory costs that we intend to isolate and analyze here. On the one hand, private equity firms operating in the European Union have an interest in translating the higher regulatory costs on investors into private equity funds and this would be consistent with the market logic according to which, typically, the increase in management costs for the service provider, the increase in the price of that service for end customers follows. On the other hand, investors in private equity funds have the opposite interest, namely to pay as little as possible for management services and thus maximize their return on capital invested in private equity funds. An analysis of the possible options follows.

a) Competitive option with costs borne by investors. If the private equity firms subject to higher regulatory costs passed the above costs onto their investors, these investors would suffer a reduction in their returns on invested capital. This would push investors to seek higher returns by investing their capital differently. The possible migration of capital would be followed by an increase in competition between the private equity firms subject to higher regulatory costs both as regards raising new funds (because it would be more difficult to obtain new capital commitments by offering lower returns), and as regards the capital investments (due to lower assets under management and reduced investment capacity). Furthermore, the reduction in the assets entrusted to the management of private equity firms subject to higher regulatory costs would be followed by a reduction in the levels of remuneration for the professionals of these private equity firms, some of which could therefore migrate to more profitable professional occupations. In short, the negative effects for private equity firms subject to higher regulatory costs would feed a negative spiral (for them), such as to make the option in question unsustainable in the long term.

b) Competitive option with costs borne by private equity firms. If the private equity firms subject to higher regulatory costs would bear the aforementioned costs, they would suffer an increase in the management costs of private equity funds and therefore would derive less profits from this activity. Consequently, professionals working for private equity firms would receive lower remuneration (since their variable remuneration is related to the profits of private equity firms) and professionals with greater experience and ability could, due to lower remuneration, migrate towards more profitable professional occupations. The mobility of the best professionals towards other occupations would cause a deterioration of the ability to create value by the private equity firms in question. This would push investors to seek higher returns by investing their capital differently. There would be a negative spiral that would make the option in question unsustainable for private equity firms. It should be noted that the option in question does not seem sustainable even for investors, since the loss of the best private equity professionals would result in a decrease in the profitability of the investments of these investors in private equity funds.

c) Cooperative option with cost sharing. The qualitative analysis of the two borderline cases set out above highlights their long-term unsustainability and suggests that private equity firms subject to higher regulatory costs share these higher costs with their private equity funds. This conclusion seems to be confirmed in a recent empirical research according to which private equity firms share the largest regulatory costs such as internal costs for 58% and costs to be transferred to investors in private equity funds for the remaining 42% [301]. The exact measure of cost sharing will reflect the negotiating balance of the parties also in light of market conditions.

The conclusions regarding the allocation of higher regulatory costs between private equity firms and investors were reached by

301 ERNST&YOUNG & PEI, *Navigating the headwinds – 2014 global private equity survey*, New York, USA, p. 7.

assuming, among other things, that the conditions of the private equity market remain stable (i.e. neutralizing them for the purposes of the previous analysis). It is now intended, however, to focus precisely on the private equity market and illustrate its possible development scenarios according to the quantity of private equity transactions (expressed in number of transactions) and the quality of private equity transactions (expressed in terms of of profitability). Four future macro-scenarios can thus be imagined.

1. In the first scenario, lower returns and less private equity transactions are assumed, for example if the structural problems of the economy worsen and the confidence of the financial markets does not stabilize[302]. In this scenario, investors would seek alternative and more profitable investments than private equity, private equity professionals would move towards alternative and more profitable professional occupations and some private equity firms would be forced to leave the market. In the scenario in question, there would be a contraction in the private equity market.

2. In the second scenario, higher returns and fewer transactions are assumed, for example in the event that there is a reduction in investment opportunities and the development of superior investment techniques/ skills by some private equity firms as a consequence of the competition between private equity firms. In this scenario, there would be strong competition between private equity firms due to the scarcity of investment opportunities with the survival of only private equity firms that have been able to develop superior investment techniques and skills. In the scenario in question, the effects on the private equity market would be mixed (on the one hand the costs and losses for the exit from the market of some private equity firms, on the other the benefits of the superior techniques/skills developed by the surviving private equity firms).

3. In the third scenario, lower returns and more transactions are assumed, for example in the event that the confidence of the financial markets and the access to financing of private equity operations are strengthened and the private equity funds have more capital available than

302 GILLIGAN J. & WRIGHT M., *Private Equity Demistified: 2012 Update*, op.cit., pp.55-56.

they can be used profitably. In this scenario, in the absence of improvements in the investment techniques/skills of private equity funds, suboptimal transactions with poor or negative returns would occur. The effects on the private equity market would be mixed (on the one hand the costs related to suboptimal operations whose returns could be low or negative, on the other the benefits of the increase in operations and investment opportunities).

4. In the fourth scenario, higher returns and more operations are assumed, for example in the case in which the confidence of the financial markets and the access to financing of private equity operations are strengthened and the private equity firms develop higher investment techniques/skills. In this scenario, market conditions would favor the conclusion of private equity transactions and private equity funds, thanks to better investment techniques or skills, would generate higher returns for their investors. A positive spiral would follow that would increase investor interest in private equity investments and consequently their capital injections to private equity funds. Therefore, in the scenario in question, there would be an expansion of the private equity market.

Returning to the options available to private equity firms for the allocation of the higher costs imposed by the new regulatory framework, it is observed that improvements in the quantity of investment opportunities (therefore in the number of private equity transactions) or in the quality of investment opportunities (therefore the profitability of private equity transactions) would push towards an allocation of higher costs for investors because it would increase the negotiating power of private equity firms. Conversely, worsening of the quantity or quality of investment opportunities would push towards the allocation of higher costs for private equity firms because it would increase the negotiating power of investors.

In conclusion, it is clear that in the absence of exogenous market development factors, the improvement and improvement of investment techniques or skills by private equity operators is the only tool for expanding the private equity market that private equity firms can control and on which it is foreseeable will focus.

6. Critical points for private equity operators

Without claiming to be exhaustive, four issues will be identified in this paragraph in relation to which it seems desirable that private equity operators take positive action for the further growth and development of the private equity market. To this end, critical points for private equity operators will be illustrated for each of these issues.

The first question concerns the growing pressure on private equity firms to review their remuneration regime which would appear exorbitant, especially in the presence of disappointing returns from their private equity funds[303]. It has already been observed that the current remuneration regime of private equity firms, the so-called "two and twenty" regime, creates a misalignment of the interests of the parties and for this reason recommendations have been suggested to mitigate this misalignment. It has also been observed that investor intolerance for the current remuneration regime of private equity firms has developed co-investment structures pari passu with the private equity fund but also these alternative structures do not seem sustainable in the long term because if generalized they would annihilate the entire economic model of private equity. In light of the above, the review of the remuneration regime of private equity firms with the aim of ensuring that this regime promotes sound and effective management of the risks assumed by private equity funds, seems to be a way in which private equity firms they can distinguish themselves positively from other operators and thus attract investors and capital[304].

The second issue concerns the growing competition between private equity firms in attracting investors. It has been observed that this is the result of a general diffusion of technical knowledge regarding private equity investments (so-called "democratization" of successes and technical knowledge). Furthermore, it has been observed that in order to continue to raise investments and capital from their investors, "private equity firms must not only achieve successful experiences but also explain how these successes have been achieved and, above all, how they will be

303 DE MARIA C., *Introduction to private equity*, op.cit., p.188 ss.

304 GHAI S., KEHOE C. & PINKUS G, *Private equity: changing perceptions and new realities*, 2014, http:// www.mckinsey.com / insights / financial_services / private_ equity_changing_perceptions_and_new_realities.

maintained"[305]. McKinsey & Company identifies the specialization of private equity firms as one of the possible development keys of the private equity market. According to recent empirical research, there is a positive correlation between the professional experience of investment managers and the returns of the portfolio companies that they supervise[306]. Specifically, the authors note that general partners whose professionals have previous experience in management or business consultancy (for example, ex-business executives or ex-strategic consultants) generate higher returns for portfolio companies concentrated in endogenous growth plans, therefore through organic development or internal reorganization plans; while general partners whose professionals have previous experience in the financial sector (for example, ex-business bankers or ex-accountants) generate higher returns for portfolio companies concentrated in exogenous growth operations, therefore with significant corporate acquisitions. The starting point for private equity firms is, therefore, to enhance their specializations by industrial area, geographical area or type of private equity intervention because the results achieved and the specializations distinguish the private equity operators from each other and, above all, this specialization seems to respond to the needs expressed by investors in selecting the private equity firms to which to confer capital under management[307].

The third question concerns the reputation of private equity and private equity firms. The main negative and positive findings regarding the economic impact of private equity have been previously illustrated and analyzed and the question of the economic impact of private equity has also been examined in the context of the debt capital market. The conclusion of the analysis is that most of the economic literature seems to

---

305 Specifically, the authors note that: "To raise capital in a newly competitive era, private-equity firms must be able not only to point to a track record of success, as in the past, but also to say how that track record was achieved and, even more critically, how it will be maintained."

306 ACHARYA V. V., GOTTSCHALG O. F., HAHN M. & KEHOE C., *Corporate Governance and Value Creation: Evidence from Private Equity*, in *The Review of Corporate Finance Studies*, vol. 26, n. 2, 2013, pp.368-402.

307 GHAI S., KEHOE C. & PINKUS G, *Private equity: changing perceptions and new realities*, 2014, available at: http://www.mckinsey.com/insights/financial_services/private_equity_changing_ perceptions_and_new_realities.

support the argument that private equity, on the whole, has a positive economic impact and that private equity would also be able to mitigate negative externalities in the corporate finance market. As already mentioned, one of the cornerstones of the regulatory reforms recently introduced in the United States and the European Union is the strengthening of transparency, not only towards regulatory authorities, but also towards investors and the market. Also in order to comply with the new regulatory obligations relating to information obligations, private equity firms should abandon the privacy screen behind which they have taken shelter - partly thanks to the absence of regulation- and take the opportunity to illustrate and demonstrate in the renewed regulatory framework introduced following the financial crisis of 2007-2008 how their superior investment techniques and skills can create value for both private equity fund investors and businesses. Once again, clear communication with investors and the market would allow virtuous private equity firms to distinguish themselves positively from others and thus attract investors and capital.

The fourth question concerns investors and their ability to select private equity funds to invest in. In order for the competition between private equity firms to be a harbinger of better investment techniques and skills (as desired above), investors must be able to recognize the private equity firms that have developed superior investment techniques and skills. To this end, it was observed that investors should equip themselves with internal resources and administrators with skills that can fully analyze and appreciate the effective capabilities of the private equity firms to which they confer capital under management[308].

7. Critical points for the legislator and regulatory authorities of the European Union

In this paragraph, without claiming to be exhaustive, three issues relating to the regulatory framework of private equity introduced into the European Union by the AIFM Directive will be identified and for each of

---

308 GHAI S., KEHOE C. & PINKUS G, *Private equity: changing perceptions and new realities*, 2014, available at: http://www.mckinsey.com/insights/financial_services/private_equity_changing_ perceptions_and_new_realities.

these issues, ideas will be formulated for the legislator and the regulatory authorities in a de jure condendo perspective.

A first critical aspect of the AIFM Directive is the "one size fits all" approach adopted by the European legislator. Specifically, private equity was attracted to the financial system reform agenda following the 2007-2008 crisis not because it was one of the contributing factors to the crisis but because it was considered that "the activities of the [private equity funds] they can contribute to spreading or amplifying risks in the financial system"[309]. The point is that private equity has been regulated like other alternative investments (for example investments by hedge funds) which are structurally different from private equity and pose systemic risks other than private equity[310]. It was noted that the intention of the European legislator was actually to take a further step towards a single European market for financial services. However, the approach adopted seems to place disproportionate burdens on the private equity industry, such as the costs of functional and hierarchical separation between the risk management functions and the investment portfolio management functions as well as the capitalization requirements[311]. It is not possible to establish whether the aforementioned higher charges are offset by the benefits envisaged by the AIFM Directive, primarily the possibility for investment fund managers to access under the "EU passport" regime in all national markets within the European Union[312]. The point is that the higher charges in question result in additional regulatory costs for private equity firms and/or investors and place private

---

309 AIFM Directive, introduction (2).

310 NABILOU H., *The Alternative Investment Fund Managers Directive and Hedge Funds' Systemic Risk Regulation in the EU*, 2013, p.91, http://papers.ssrn.com/sol3/papers.cfm?abstract_id=2352373.

311 ERNST&YOUNG, *Game-changing regulation? The perceived impact of the AIFM Directive on private equity in Europe*, New York, USA, 2012, p.6, http://www.ey.com/Publication/vwLUAssets/The_perceived_impact_of_the_AIFM_Directive_on_private_equity_in_Europe/$FILE/AIFMD_European_inpact_survey.pdf.

312 According to a survey conducted among private equity operators, albeit balancing pro and contra of the AIFM Directive, 72% of operators fear that the AIFM Directive represents more of a threat than an opportunity, see: DELOITTE, *Responding to the new reality – Alternative Investment Fund Managers Directive Survey*, New York, USA, 2012, p.6, http://www.deloitte.com/assets/Dcom- BruneiDarussalam/Local%20 Assets/Documents/Financial%20Services/Alternative%20Investment %20Fund%20 Managers%20Directive%20Responding%20to%20the%20new%20reality.pdf.

equity firms operating in the European Union in a disadvantageous position compared to the others[313]. A review of the regulatory framework that takes account of the specific features of private equity and differentiates it from other alternative investment classes would therefore be desirable, for example by reviewing the charges of functional and hierarchical separation between risk management and management functions of the investment portfolio as well as the capitalization requirements.

A second critical aspect concerns some disclosure obligations envisaged in the event that the investment fund acquires control of an unlisted company. These communications are expected to be borne by the managers of alternative investment funds and, albeit indirectly, in favor of the workers of the companies being acquired. Specifically, the fund manager is required to indicate, among other things, his intentions in relation to the future activity of the unlisted company being acquired and the likely repercussions on employment, including any significant change in the working conditions of the workers of that company[314]. The disclosure obligations in question appear problematic for various reasons. First, they would require the disclosure of intra-corporate information, typically contained in the management plan and confidential, thus placing investment fund managers in a disadvantageous position in the market for the acquisition of corporate control[315]. The point is that these obligations could make the corporate control market less efficient by discouraging interventions by fund managers subject to the disclosure obligations in question. The second critical profile concerns the potential competitive damage for the company being acquired because competitors of that company may become aware of the aforementioned intra-company information. In the light of the foregoing, it would be desirable to revise the regulatory framework aimed at protecting the confidentiality of intra-

313 NABILOU H., *The Alternative Investment Fund Managers Directive and Hedge Funds' Systemic Risk Regulation in the EU*, op.cit., p.91. SERETAKIS A., *A comparative examination of private equity in the United States and Europe: accounting for the past and predicting the future*, op.cit., p.660.

314 AIFM Directive (2011/61/EU), art. 28 (4).

315 It is intended to refer to the "intentions [of the manager of the alternative investment fund] in relation to the future activity of the unlisted company [subject of acquisition] and the likely repercussions on employment."

corporate information in order to avoid altering the balance in the corporate control market.

A third critical aspect, for reasons similar to the previous one, concerns the anti-unbundling provisions of the AIFM Directive according to which, in the twenty-four months following the acquisition of control of a company (listed or not), investment fund managers cannot carry out certain operations on the capital of this company[316]. Even such restrictions, such as the disclosure obligations in the event of the purchase of control previously illustrated, would place investment fund managers in a disadvantageous position in the market for the acquisition of corporate control. Once again, the point is that the forecasts in question could make the corporate control market less efficient by discouraging interventions by fund managers subject to the anti-unbundling provisions in question. Also with reference to the latter critical profile, a review of the regulatory framework would be desirable to eliminate this difference in treatment and ensure a common level of charges and rules in the corporate control market.

316 AIFM Directive (2011/61/EU), premise (57) and art. 30.

CONCLUSIONS

The private equity sector has reached such dimensions that it is a relevant factor of modern capitalism. This explains the interest of operators, academics, legislators and regulatory authorities. Also in order to contribute to the deepening of technical knowledge for a sustainable development of private equity, this work has been articulated in an economic analysis of private equity and a comparative analysis of private equity regulation in the United States and in the Union European. Based on the aforementioned analyzes, recommendations have been proposed and critical ideas have been developed for operators, legislators and regulatory authorities, as briefly summarized below.

An examination of the remuneration policies and practices of private equity firms revealed that current market terms create a misalignment between the interests of private equity firms and the interests of investors. In particular, private equity firms could receive exorbitant compensation even if the returns for their investors were negative or lower than expected. Furthermore, private equity firms may have incentives to take excessive risks in the management of the investment portfolio as well as to accelerate or delay investments or divestments contrary to the interests of investors. In order to mitigate this interest misalignment, specific changes were made to the economic terms and the structure of the management fees, the performance fees, the direct investment of the general partner in the private equity fund as well as the other fees in favor of private equity firms.

The complex issue of the economic impact of private equity was also examined, analyzing and systematising the scientific contributions published on this issue in the past twenty years. Although opposite positions are not lacking, according to the majority doctrine private equity has (i) produced higher returns for investors in private equity funds, (ii) generated profits for private equity firms, and (iii) favored managerial, operational and in the field of portfolio company innovation; overall, private equity is a phenomenon with a positive net economic effect, that is, private equity creates value. However, the above scientific contributions appear to be limited by the quantity and quality of the underlying data as well as by the analysis methodologies adopted. The conclusions reached by the economic literature must therefore be contextualized within the limits identified in this work.

Regardless of the conclusions reached by the economic literature on the economic impact of private equity, an innovative thesis was presented and demonstrated that private equity firms would play a positive role in the debt capital market: They would mitigate some typical agency costs of the market of debt capital, would facilitate the meeting between demand and supply of loans to its portfolio companies and, in this way, would contribute to the influx of capital at the service of the real economy.

Furthermore, to support this thesis, the major sectors were analyzed where the most important private equity firms operate globally, namely that of infrastructure and environmental sustainability.

As for the analysis of private equity regulation in the United States and the European Union, the two regulatory frameworks were first reconstructed and a comparative analysis of the same was then developed. From this comparative analysis it emerged that European regulation imposes higher charges for private equity firms and this translates into higher regulatory costs. Therefore, three options for the allocation of the higher regulatory costs were hypothesized and examined and it was demonstrated that both the transfer of the higher costs to investors in private equity funds, and the absorption of the costs in question by private equity firms are unsustainable options in the long term because, respectively, they would push investors to look for alternative and more profitable private equity investments or they would cause the best private equity professionals to escape, with a consequent reduction in the ability of private equity firms to create value. It was therefore concluded that the higher regulatory costs should be shared between private equity firms and investors. The quantity and quality of private equity investment opportunities on the market are the variables that will define the extent of the distribution of the aforementioned higher regulatory costs between private equity firms and investors, as well as the future scenarios of the private equity sector.

In the light of the economic analysis of private equity and the comparative analysis of private equity regulation in the United States and the European Union, critical ideas have been proposed for a sustainable development of the sector in question. Specifically, private equity firms are suggested to review their remuneration policies and practices according to the recommendations proposed for better alignment of the parties' interests, to pursue specialization strategies by industrial area, geographical area or type of private equity intervention to meeting the needs of its investors and, finally, improving its communication strategies to demonstrate, in the light of the new regulatory framework and the new and more stringent information and transparency obligations, their skills and techniques for creating value. Instead, it was suggested to private equity investors to equip themselves with suitable resources to fully analyze the capabilities of private equity firms, so that the competition between private equity firms is actually heralding improvements in investment skills and techniques. Finally, it has been suggested to the European legislator and to the regulatory authorities to review some specific provisions of the AIFM Directive (for example the disclosure obligations in the event of the purchase of control of an unlisted company and the anti-unbundling rules) which seem to hinder the investments of private equity making the corporate control market less efficient. The forecasts in question place greater burdens on certain private equity firms than other operators in the corporate control market (such as captive funds, sovereign wealth funds or, more simply, industrial operators not subject to the AIFM Directive) by altering competition.

In conclusion, the growing need for capital to serve long-term business projects and the current fragility of the traditional system of business financing (banks and capital markets) represent clear development opportunities for the private equity sector. The challenge for the sector will not only be to seize these opportunities, but also to critically review its economic model, starting with the remunerative policies and practices of private equity firms. Legislators and regulatory authorities are left with the task of recognizing and enhancing the specificity of private equity and building a regulatory framework appropriate to the global dimension that the phenomenon has now reached.

BIBLIOGRAPHY

ACHARYA V. & RICHARDSON M., *Restoring financial stability: how to repair a failed system*, New York, USA, New York University Stern School of Business, 2009.

ACHARYAV. V., FRANKS J. & SERVAES H., *Private Equity: Boom and Bust?*, in *Journal of Applied Corporate Finance*, vol. 19, n. 4, 2007, pp.44–53.

ACHARYA V.V., GOTTSHALG O. F., HAHN M. & KEHOE C., *Corporate Governance and Value Creation: Evidence from Private Equity*, in *The Review of Corporate Finance Studies*, vol. 26, n. 2, 2013, pp.368-402.

AIFI, *Capitali per lo sviluppo – Sesto rapporto Biennale 1997-1998*, Milan, Italy, Guerini e Associati, 1997.

AIFI, *L'investimento in un fondo di private equity: guida al processo di selezione e due diligence,* 2012.

AKERLOF G. A., *The Market for "Lemons:" Quality Uncertainty and the Market Mechanism*, in *The Quarterly Journal of Economics*, vol. 84, n. 3., 1970, pp.488-500.

ALBANESE A., *Leveraged buy out, rifinanziamento del debito originario e costituzione di garanzie reali*, in *Nuova giur. civ. comm.*, vol. II, 2006.

AMESS K. & WRIGHT M., *Barbarians at the Gate? Leveraged Buyouts, Private Equity and Jobs*, in *Nottingham University Business School Research Paper Series*, 2007, available at: http://papers.ssrn.com/sol3/papers.cfm?abstract_id=1034178.

AMESS K., BROWN S. & THOMPSON S., *Management Buyouts, Supervision and Employee Discretion*, in *Scottish Journal of Political Economy*, vol. 54, n. 4, 2007, pp.447-474.

AMESS K., GIRMA, S. & WRIGHT M., *What are the Wage and Employment Consequences of Leveraged Buyouts, Private Equity and Acquisitions in the UK?*, in *Nottingham University Business School Research Paper*, n. 2008-01, 2008, available at: http://papers.ssrn.com/sol3/papers.cfm?abstract_id=1270581.

AMESS K., *Management buy-outs and firm-level productivity: evidence from a panel of UK Manufacturing Firms*, in *Scottish Journal of Political Economy*, vol. 49, 2002, pp.304-317.

AMESS K., *The effects of management buy-outs and on firm-level technical efficiency: evidence from a panel of UK machinery and equipment manufacturers*, in *Journal of Industrial Economics*, vol. 51, 2003, pp.35-44.

ANDEADE G. & KAPLAN S., *How costly is financial (not economic) distress? Evidence from highly leveraged transactions that became distressed*, in *Journal of Finance*, vol. 53, 1998, pp.1443-1493.

ANNUAL REPORT 2019, *European PE Breakdown*, PitchBook, 2020.

ANTONELLI G., *Crasso, il banchiere di Roma*, Rome, Italy, Newton, 1995.

ARMOUR J., *Legal Capital: an Outdated Concept?*, in *Centre for Business Research – University of Cambridge*, Working Paper n. 320, 2006, available at: http://www.cbr.cam.ac.uk/pdf/WP320.pdf.

ATANASOV V., IVANOV V. & LITVAK K., *Does Reputation Limit Opportunistic Behavior in the VC Industry? Evidence from Litigation against VCs*, in *Journal of Finance*, vol. 67, n. 6, 2012, pp.2215-2246.

AWREY D., *The Limits of EU Hedge Fund Regulation*, in *Oxford Legal Studies – Research Paper*, n. 8/2011, 2011, available at: http://papers.ssrn.com/sol3/papers.cfm?abstract_id=1757719.

AXELSON U., JENKINSON T., STRÖMBERG P. & WEISBACH S., *Borrow Cheap, Buy High?*, in *The Journal of Finance*, vol. 68, n. 6, 2013, pp.2223–2267.

AXELSON U., SRÖMBERG P. & WEISBACH S., *Why Are Buyouts Levered? The Financial Structure of Private Equity Funds*, in *The Journal of Finance*, vol. 64, n. 4, 2009, pp.1549-1582.

BACON N., WRIGHT M. & DEMINA N., *Management Buyouts and Human Resource Management*, in *British Journal of Industrial Relations*, vol. 42, n. 2, 2004, pp.325-347.

BACON N., WRIGHT M., MEULEMAN M. & SCHOLES L., *The impact of private equity on management practices in European buy-outs: Short-termism, Anglo-Saxon or host country effects?' Industrial Relations*, in *Industrial Relations: A Journal of Economy and Society*, vol. 51, 2011, pp.605-626.

BAKER G. P. & SMITH G. D., *The New Financial Capitalists – Kohlberg Kravis Roberts and the Creation of Corporate Value*, Cambridge, UK, Cambridge University Press, 1998.

BAKS K. P. & BENVENISTE L. M., *Alignment of Interest in the Private Equity Industry*, in *Emory Center for Alternative Investments papers*, 2010, available at: http://goizueta.emory.edu/Faculty/cai/documents/ECAI_Alignment.pdf.

BARBA V., *Profili civilistici del leveraged buy out*, Milan, Italy, Giuffrè, 2003.

BARBERIS N. & THALER R., *A Survey of Behavioral Finance*, in *Handbook of the Economics of Finance* (ed.by Constantinides G., Harris M. & Stulz R.), Amsterdam, Holland, Elsevier, 2013.

BARTLETT J., *Fundamentals of Venture Capital*, Lanham, USA, Madison Books, 1999.

BARTLETT R. P., *Taking Finance Seriously: How Debt Financing Distorts Bidding Outcomes in Corporate Takeovers*, in *Fordham Law Review*, vol. 76, 2008, pp.1975-2026.

BAUMOL W.J., OATES W., "*The Theory of Environmental Policy.*" Cambridge University Press, Cambridge, 1988.

BEBCHUK L. A. & FRIED J. M., *Executive Compensation as an Agency Problem*, in *Journal of Economic Perspectives*, vol. 17, n. 3, 2003, pp.71-92.

BEBCHUK L. A. & FRIED J. M., *Executive Compensation at Fannie Mae: A Case Study of Perverse Incentives, Nonperformance Pay, and Camouflage*, in *Journal of Corporation Law*, vol. 30, n. 4, 2005, pp.807-822.

BEBCHUK L. A. & FRIED J. M., *Pay without Performance: Overview of the Issues*, in *Journal of Corporation Law*, vol. 30, n. 4, 2005, pp.647-673.

BEN-DAVID I., GRAHAM J. R. & CAMPBELL R. H., *Managerial Overconfidence and Corporate Policies*, in *NBER Working Paper*, n. 13711, 2007.

BERGMANN B., CHRISTOPHERS H., HUSS M. & ZIMMERMANN H., *Listed Private Equity*, in *Private Equity: Fund Types, Risks and Returns, and Regulation* (ed.by Cumming D. J.), Hoboken, USA, John Wiley & Sons, 2009, pp.53- 70.

BERNSTEIN S., LERNER J., SØRENSEN M. & STRÖMBERG P., *Private Equity and Industry Performance*, in *NBER Working Paper*, n. 15632, 2010.

BLOOD, D. in "*The case for sustainable business*," Gresham College, 21 January 2008.

BLOOM N., VAN REENEN J., SADUN R., *Do private equity-owned firms have better management practices*, in *The Global Economic Impact of Private Equity Report 2009 – Globalization of Alternative Investments – Working Papers* (ed.by Gurung A. & Lerner J.), vol. 2, World Economic Forum, 2009, pp.47-64.

BODIE M. T., *Mother Jones Meets Gordon Gekko: The Complicated Relationship between Labor and Private Equity*, in *Colorado Law Review*, vol. 79, n. 4, 2008, pp.1317-1354.

BORELL M. & TYKVOVA T., *Do Private Equity Investors Trigger Financial Distress in Their Portfolio Companies?*, in *Journal of Corporate Finance*, vol. 18, n. 1, 2012, pp.138-150.

BOUCLY Q., THESMAR D. & SRAER D., *Leveraged buy-outs – evidence from French deals'*, in *The Global Economic Impact of Private Equity Report 2009 – Globalization of Alternative Investments – Working Papers* (ed.by Gurung A. & Lerner J.), vol. 2, World Economic Forum, 2009, pp.47-64.

BREALEY R. A., MYERS S. C. & ALLEN F., *Principles of Corporate Finance. Global Edition*, New York, USA, McGraw-Hill/Irwin, 2011.

BRIGHAM E.F., HOUSTON J.F., *Fundamentals of Financial Management,* South-Western Pub, concise edition, 2019.

BROWN D. T., FEE C. E. & THOMAS S. E., *Financial leverage and bargaining power with suppliers: Evidence from leveraged buy-outs*, in *Journal of Corporate Finance*, vol. 15, n. 2, 2009, pp.196-211.

BROWN G.W., GREDIL O.R., KAPLAN S.N., *Do private equity funds manipulate reported returns?*, in *Journal of Financial Economics*, 132 (2), 2019, pp. 269ss.

BRUINING H. & WRIGHT M., *Entrepreneurial orientation in management buyouts and the contribution of venture capital*, in *Venture Capital: An International Journal of Entrepreneurial Finance*, vol. 4, 2002, pp.147-168.

BRUINING H., BONNET M. & WRIGHT M., *Management control systems and strategy change in buy-outs*, in *Management Accounting Research*, vol. 15, 2004, pp.155- 177.

BRUINING H., WRIGHT M., BOSELIE P. & BACON N., *The Impact of Business Ownership Change on Employee Relations: Buy-Outs in the UK and the Netherlands*, in *ERIM Report*, Series Reference n. ERS-2004-021-ORG, 2004,available at: http://papers.ssrn.com/sol3/papers.cfm?abstract_id=797249.

BRUTON G., KEELS J. K. & SCIFRES R. L., *Corporate restructuring and performance: an agency perspective on the complete buy-out cycle*, in *Journal of Business Research*, vol. 55, 20002, pp.709-724.

BURROUGH B. & HELYAR J., *Barbarians at the Gate. The Fall of RJR Nabisco*, New York, USA, HarperCollins Publishers, 2008.

BYGRAVE W. D., HAY M. & PEETERS J.B., *Realizing Investment Value*, London, UK, Pitman Publishing, 1994.

CAFARO R., *Il merchant banking*, in *I singoli contratti – Applicazioni pratiche; clausole specifiche; giurisprudenza di riferimento* (ed.by G. Cassano), Padua, Italy, Cedam, 2010.

CAMPOBASSO G. F., *Diritto Commerciale – Diritto delle Società*, vol. 2, Milanofiori Assago, Italy, Wolters Kluwer Italia, 2012.

CANALE ENERGIA, *Dall'UE 800 mln di euro per infrastrutture energetiche prioritarie. I finanziamenti rientrano nel Connecting Europe Facility*, 29 January 2019.

CAO J. & LERNER J., *The Performance of Reverse Leveraged Buyouts*, in *NBER Working Paper*, n. 12626, 2006, available at: http://www.nber.org/papers/w12626.

CASELLI S, GARCIA-APPENDINI E. & IPPOLITO F., *Explaining Returns in Private Equity Investments*, in *CAREFIN Working Paper*, n. 15/09, 2009, available at: http://www.rcfea.org/papers_sme/paper_Caselli.pdf.

CASELLI S., *Private Equity and Venture Capital in Europe: Markets, Techniques, and Deals*, Oxford, UK, Academic Press, 2010.

CENDROWSKI H., MARTIN J., PETRO L. & WADECKI A., *Private Equity: History, Governance and Operations*, Chichester, UK, John Wiley & Sons, 2008.

CHEFFINS B. & ARMOUR J., *The Eclipse of Private Equity*, in *ECGI – Law Working Paper*, n. 082/2007, 2007.

CHERTOK S., *A comprehensive guide to Title IV of the Dodd-Frank Act and the rules promulgated thereunder*, in *UC Davis Business Law Journal*, vol. 12, 2012, pp.125-223.

CHOI S., *Market Lessons for Gatekeepers*, in *Northwestern University Law Review*, vol. 92, n. 4, 1998, pp.934-949.

CITRON D., WRIGHT M., *Bankruptcy costs, leverage & multiple secured creditors: the case of MBOs*, in *Accounting and Business Research*, vol. 38, n. 1, 2008, pp.71-90.

CITRON D., WRIGHT M., RIPPINGTON F. & BALL R., *Secured creditor recovery rates from management buy-outs in distress*, in *European Financial Management*, vol. 9, n. 2, 2003, pp.141-162.

CIVERRA E., *Le operazioni di fusione e scissione – L'impatto della riforma e la nuova disciplina del leveraged buy out*, Milan, Italy, IPSOA, 2003.

CLAESSENS S., KOSE M. A., LAEVEN L. & VALENCIA F., *Financial Crises: Causes, Consequences, and Policy Responses*, Washington D.C., USA, International Monetary Fund, 2014.

CLARK,G.L. & ROOT,A., *Infrastructure shortfall in the United Kingdom: the private finance initiative and government policy*, in *Political Geography* , vol.18, 1999, pp. 341-365.

COFFEE J. C., *Gatekeeper Failure and Reform: The Challenge of Fashioning Relevant Reforms*, in *Boston University Law Review,* vol. 84, 2004, pp.301–64.

CONSOB, *Relazione sull'attività di Analisi di Impatto della Regolamentazione – Attuazione della Direttiva sui gestori di fondi di investimento alternativi (AIFMD)*, 2014.

COOTER R., MATTEI U., MONATERI P. G., PARDOLESI R. & ULEN T., *Il mercato delle regole – Analisi economica del diritto civile*, Bologna,Italy, Il Mulino, 2006.

CORNELLI F., KARAKAS O., *Private equity and corporate governance: do LBOs have more effective boards?*, in *The Global Impact of Private Equity Report 2008 – Globalization of Alternative Investments – Working Papers* (ed. by Lerner J. & Gurung A.), vol. 1, Geneva, Switzerland, World Economic Forum, 2008, pp.65-84.

COVITZ D. & LIANG N., *Recent Development in the Private Equity Market and the Role of Preferred Returns*, Mimeo, 2002, available at: http://www.bis.org/publ/cgfs19board1.pdf.

CRAIG P. & DE BURCA G., *EU Law – Text, Cases, and Materials*, Oxford, UK, Oxford University Press, 2011.

CRESSY R., MUNARI F. & MALIPIERO A., *Playing to their strengths? Evidence that specialization in the Private Equity industry confers competitive advantage*, in *Journal of Corporate Finance*, vol. 13, n. 4, 2007, pp.647-669.

CUMMING D. & WALZ U., *Private Equity Returns and Disclosure around the World*, in *LSE RICAFE – Working Paper*, n. 9, 2004, available at: http://www.lse.ac.uk/fmg/research/RICAFE/pdf/RICAFE-WP09-Cumming.pdf.

CUMMING D. J. & ZAMBELLI S., *Illegal buy-outs*, in *Journal of Banking and Finance*, vol. 34, 2010, pp.441-456.

DAMIANI E., *Venture Capital e Private Equity*, Naples, Italy, Edizioni Scientifiche Italiane, 2010.

DAMODARAN A., *The Anatomy of an LBO: Leverage, Control and Value*, 2008, available at: http://papers.ssrn.com/sol3/papers.cfm?abstract_id=1162862.

DAVIS S. J., HALTIWANGER J. C., JARMIN R. S., LERNER J. & MIRANDA J., *Private equity and employment*, in *The Global Impact of Private Equity Report 2008 – Globalization of Alternative Investments – Working Papers* (ed.by Lerner J. & Gurung A.), vol. 1, Geneva,Switzerland, World Economic Forum, 2008, pp. 43- 64.

DE CECCO M. & FERRI G., *Origini e natura speciale dell'attività di banca d'affari in Italia*, in *Banca d'Italia – Temi di discussione del Servizio studi*, vol. 242, 1994.

DE FONTENAY E., *Private Equity Firms As Gatekeepers*, in *Review of Banking & Financial Law*, vol. 33, 2013, pp.115-189.

DE MAESENEIRE W. & BRINKHUIS S., *What drives leverage in leveraged buyouts? An analysis of European leveraged buyouts' capital structure*, in *Accounting & Finance*, vol. 52, n. 1s, 2012, pp.155-182.

DE MARIA C., *Introduction to private equity*, Chichester, UK, John Wiley & Sons Ltd., 2010.

DELOITTE, *2013 Private Equity Fund Outlook*, New York, USA, 2012, available at: http://www2. deloitte.com / content / dam / Deloitte / global / Documents/ Financial Services/dttl- fsi-US-FSI-2013PEOutlook-121912.pdf.

DELOITTE, *Responding to the new reality – Alternative Investment Fund Managers Directive Survey*, New York, USA, 2012, available at: http://www. deloitte.com/assets/Dcom-BruneiDarussalam/Local%20Assets/Documents/ Financial%20Services/Alternative%20Investment%20Fund%20Managers% 20Directive%20Responding%20to%20the%20new%20reality.pdf.

DEMIROGLU C. & JAMES C. M., *Lender control and the role of private equity group reputation in buyout financing*, in *Journal of Financial Economics*, vol. 96, 2010, pp.306-330.

DILLER C. & KASERER C., *What Drives Private Equity Returns?– Fund Inflows, Skilled GPs, and/or Risk?*, in *European Financial Management*, vol. 15, n. 3, 2009, pp.643-675.

DRIESSEN J., LIN T. & PHALIPPOU L., *Estimating the Performance and Risk Exposure of Private Equity Funds: A New Methodology*, in *NETSPAR Discussion Paper*, n.23,2007.

EASTERWOD J. C., *Divestments and financial distress in leveraged buyouts*, in *Journal of Banking & Finance*, vol. 22, n. 2, 1998, pp.129-159.

ERNST&YOUNG & PEI, *Navigating the headwinds – 2014 global private equity survey*,New York, USA, 2014.

ERNST&YOUNG, *Game-changing regulation? The perceived impact of the AIFM Directive on private equity in Europe*, New York, USA, 2012, available at: http://www.ey.com/Publication/vwLUAssets/The_perceived_ impact_of_the_AFM_Directive_on_private_equity_in_Europe/$FILE/AIF MD_European_inpact_survey.pdf.

ESTY B. C., *The economic motivations for using Project Finance,* in *Mimeo*, 2003.

EUROPEAN COMMISSION, *Commission staff working document – Economic Review of the Financial Regulation Agenda*, SWD(2014) 158 final, 2014.

EUROPEAN COMMISSION, *Press release – Directive on Alternative Investment Fund Managers ('AIFMD'): Frequently Asked Questions*, Memo/ 10/572, 2011.

EUROPEAN ENVIRONMENT AGENCY, *Climate change mitigation. Trends and projections in Europe 2019. The EU Emissions Trading System in 2019: trends and projections*, 31 October 2019.

EUROSIF, *European SRI Study,* 2018.

EVCA, *European Private Equity Activity Data 2007-2013*, in *EVCA Research*, 2014.

EVCA, *Private Equity Fund Structures in Europe*, in *EVCA Research*, 2006.

EVCA, *Private Equity Fund Structures in Europe*, in *EVCA Research*, 2010.

EWANG F. N., *An Analysis and Critique of the European Union's Minimum Capitalization Requirement*, in *Charles Sturt University (Australia) Working Papers*, 2007, available at: http://papers.ssrn.com/sol3/papers.cfm?abstract_id=1015708.

EWENS M., JONES C. M. & RHODES-KROPF M., *The Price of Diversifiable Risk in Venture Capital and Private Equity*, in *Oxford Journals – The Review of Financial Studies*, vol. 26, n. 8, 2013, pp.1854-1889.

FENN G. W., LIANG N. & PROWSE S., *The Private Equity Market: An Overview*, in *Financial Markets, Institutions, and Instruments*, vol. 6, n. 4., 1997, pp.1-106.

FRIGNANI A., *Il leveraged Buy-Out nel diritto italiano*, in *Giur. comm.*, vol. I, 1989, pp.419-429.

FRIGNANI A., voce *Leveraged buyout*, in *Dig. disc. priv., sez. comm.*, IX, Torino, Italy, Utet, 1993.

FRIGNANI A., voce *Venture Capital*, in *Noviss. Dig. It.*, App. VII, Torino, Italy, 1987.

FRONTIER ECONOMICS, *Exploring the impact of private equity on economic growth in Europe*, London, UK, Frontier Economics Ltd, 2013, p.32 ss., available at: https://www.evca.eu/media/12929/Frontier-Economics- Report.pdf.

FUDENBERG D. & TIROLE J., *Game Theory*, Cambridge, USA, The MIT Press, 1991.

GANDHI V.S., BRUMME C.R., MEHTA S., "*The Rise Fund: TPG Bets Big on Impact,*" in *Harvard Business School* case 318-041, February 2018 (revised August 2019).

GASPAR J., *The Performance of French LBO Firms: New data and new results*, in *ESSEC Working Paper*, 2009.

GERVASONI A. & SATTIN F. L., *Private equity e venture capital – Manuale di investimento nel capitale di rischio*, Milan, Italy, Guerini Studio, 2008.

GERVASONI A., *Finanziarie l'attività imprenditoriale*, Milan, Italy, Guerini Associati, 1996.

GHAI S., KEHOE C. & PINKUS G, *Private equity: changing perceptions and new realities*, 2014, available at: http://www.mckinsey.com/insights/financial_services/private_equity_changing_perceptions_and_new_realities.

GILLIGAN J. & WRIGHT M., *Private Equity Demistified: 2012 Update*, London, UK, The Institute of Chartered Accountants in England and Wales, 2012.

GILLIGAN J. & WRIGHT M., *Private Equity Demistified: An Explanatory Guide*, London, UK, The Institute of Chartered Accountants in England and Wales, 2008.

GINEVRA E., *Oltre il capitale sociale? Spunti per la ripresa del dibattito sulla riforma della struttura finanziaria delle società di capitali*, in *La struttura finanziaria e i bilanci delle società di capitali – Studi in onore di Giovanni E. Colombo* (ed. by Aa. Vv.), Torino, Italy, Giappichelli, 2011, 3 ss.

GIULIANO G., *Fusione con indebitamento e leveraged buy out*, in *Notariato*, vol. 3, 2007, pp.319-327.

GLOBAL PRIVATE EQUITY REPORT 2019, Bain & Company, Boston, Massachusetts-USA, pp.7-8.

GOERGEN M., O'SULLIVAN N. & WOOD G., *Private Equity Takeovers and Employment in the UK: Some Empirical Evidence*, in *ECGI Working Paper Series in Finance*, n. 310/2011, 2011.

GONG J. & WU S., *CEO turnover in private equity sponsored leveraged buy-outs*, in *Corporate Governance: An International Review*, vol. 19, n. 3, 2011, pp. 195-209.

GOSPEL H., PENDLETON A., VITOLS S. & WILKE P., *New Investment Funds, Restructuring, and Labor Outcomes: A European Perspective*, in *Corporate Governance: An International Review*, vol. 19, n. 3, 2011, pp.276-289.

GOTTSCHALG O., PHALIPPOU L. & ZOLLO M., *Performance of Private Equity Funds: Another Puzzle?*, in *INSEAD-Wharton Alliance Center for Global Research & Development Working Paper Series*, n. 2004/82/SM/ACGRD 6, 2004.

GOTTSCHALG O., *Private Equity and Leveraged Buy-outs*, European Parliament, Study IP/A/ECON/IC/2007-25, 2007, available at: http://www.europarl.europa.eu/RegData/etudes/etudes/join/2007/393515/IPOLECON_ET%282007%29393515_EN.pdf.

GREENWOOD D. J. H., *Democracy and Delaware: The Mysterious Race to the Top/Bottom*, in *Yale Law and Policy Review*, vol. 23, 2005, pp.381-454.

GREENWOOD D. J. H., *Looting: the puzzle of private equity*, in *Brooklyn Journal of Financial and Commercial Law*, vol. 3, 2008, pp.89-125.

GROH A. & GOTTSCHALG O., *The risk-adjusted performance of US buy-outs*, in *HEC Working Paper*, 2006.

GUO S., HOTCHKISS E. & SONG, W., *Do buy-outs (Still) create value?*, in *Journal of Finance*, vol. 66, 2011, pp.479-517.

GUPTA U., *The First Venture Capitalist*, Calgary, Canada, Gondolier, 2004.

HARRIS L., *A Critical Theory of Private Equity*, in *Delaware Journal of Corporate Law*, vol. 35, 2010, pp.259-293.

HARRIS R., SIEGEL D.S. & WRIGHT M., *Assessing the impact of management buyouts on economic efficiency: plant-level evidence from the United Kingdom*, in *The Review of Economics and Statistics*, vol. 87, 2005, pp.148-153.

HEALY P. M. & PALEPU K. G., *Information asymmetry, corporate disclosure, and the capital markets: A review of the empirical disclosure literature*, in *Journal of Accounting and Economics*, vol. 31, 2001, pp.405–440.

HEGE U., LOVO S., SLOVIN M., SUSHKA M., *The role of private equity in corporate asset sales: Theory and evidence*, paper presented at ESSEC 2nd Private Equity Conference, Paris, 2009.

HENDERSON M. T. & EPSTEIN R. A., *Introduction to 'The Going Private Phenomenon: Causes and Implications'*, in *The University of Chicago Law & Economics –Olin Working Paper*, n. 430, 2008, available at: http://papers.ssrn.com/sol3/papers.cfm?abstract_id=1269524.

HILL K.F., *Infrastructure funds on the rise*, January/February 2008, www.renewcanada.net ReNew Canada.

HOTCHKISS E. S., SMITH D. C. & STRÖMBERG P., *Private Equity and the Resolution of Financial Distress*, in *ECGI - Finance Working Paper*, n. 331/2012, 2012.

HSU D. & KENNEDY M., *Organizing Venture Capital: the Rise and Demise of American Research & Development Corporation, 1946-1973*, in *Industrial and Corporate Change*, vol. 14, 2005, pp.579-616.

HUNT J. P., *Credit Rating Agencies and the 'Worldwide Credit Crisis': The Limits of Reputation, the Insufficiency of Reform, and a Proposal for Improvement*, in Columbia Business Law Review, vol. 1, n. 1, 2009, pp.109-209.

IANNOTTA, G., *Investment Banking – A Guide to Underwriting and Advisory Services*, Berlin, Germany, Springer-Verlag, 2010.

ILPA, *Private Equity Principles*, v. 2.0, 2011, available at: http://ilpa.org/ilpa-private-equity-principles/.

IMPERATORI G., *"Il project financing: una tecnica, una cultura, una politica,"* Milan, Italy, Il Sole 24 Ore, 1995.

IVASHINA V. & KOVNER A., *The Private Equity Advantage: Leveraged Buyout Firms and Relationship Banking*, in *The Review of Financial Studies*, vol. 24, n. 7, 2011, pp.2462-2498.

JAFFE, A. B, et al, *"Environmental Regulation and the competitiveness of U.S. manufacturing: What does the evidence tell Us?,"* in *Journal of Economic Literature*, vol.33, 1995, pp. 132-163.

JELIC R. & WRIGHT M., *Exits, performance, and late stage private equity: The case of UK management buy-outs*, in *European Financial Management*, vol. 17, 2011, pp.560-593.

JELIC R., *Staying Power of UK Buy-Outs*, in *Journal of Business Finance & Accounting*, vol. 38, n. 7-8, 2011, pp.945-986.

JENSEN M. C. & MECKLING W. H., *Theory of the Firm: Managerial Behavior, Agency Costs and Ownership Structure*, in *Journal of Financial Economics*, vol. 3, n. 4, 1976, pp.305-360.

JENSEN M. C., *Eclipse of the Public Corporation*, in *Harvard Business Review*, 1989.

JENSEN M. C., KAPLAN S. N. & STIGLIN L., *Effects of LBOs on Tax Revenues of the U.S. Treasury*, in *Tax Notes*, vol. 42, n. 6, 1989.

JENSEN, M. C., *Agency Cost Of Free Cash Flow, Corporate Finance, and Takeovers*, in *American Economic Review*, vol. 76, n. 2, 1986, pp.323-329.

KAHNEMAN D. & LOVALLO D., *Timid Choices and Bold Forecasts: A Cognitive Perspective on Risk Taking*, in *Management Science*, vol. 39, n. 1, 1993, pp.17-31.

KAHNEMAN, D., KNETSCH, J. L., & THALER, R. H., *Experimental Tests of the Endowment Effect and the Coase Theorem*, in *Journal of Political Economy*, vol. 98, n. 6, 1990, pp.1325-1348.

KAPLAN S. & SCHOAR A., *Private Equity Performance: Returns, Persistence, and Capital Flows*, in *The Journal of Finance*, vol. LX, n. 4, 2005, pp.1791-1823.

KAPLAN S. & STRÖMBERG P., *Leveraged Buyouts and Private Equity*, in *Journal of Economic Perspectives*, vol. 23, n. 1, 2009, pp.121-146.

KAPLAN S. N., *The effects of management buy-outs on operations and value*, in *Journal of Financial Economics*, vol. 24, n. 2, 1989, pp.217-254.

KITTREDGE G. & PAUL T., *The AIFM Directive vs. Dodd-Frank – Comparative Strenghts and Weaknesses*, Mimeo, 2011.

KLAUSNER M., *Institutional Shareholders, Private Equity, and Antitakeover Protection at the IPO Stage*, in *University of Pennsylvania Law Review*, vol. 152, 2003, pp.755-784.

KNIGGE A., NOWAK E. & SCHMIDT D., *On the Performance of Private Equity Investments: Does Market Timing Matter?*, in *Journal of Financial Transformation*, vol. 16, 2006,pp. 123-134.

LAWLESS H.T., HEYMANN H., *Sensory evaluation of food: principles and practices*, 2nd edition, New York, USA, Springer, 2010.

LERNER J, SCHOAR A. & WONGSUNWAI W., *Smart Institutions, Foolish Choices: The Limited Partner Performance Puzzle*, in *The Journal of Finance*, vol. 62, n. 2, 2007, pp.731-764.

LERNER J., STRÖMBERG P. & SØRENSEN M., *Private equity and long-run investment: the case of innovation*, in *The Global Impact of Private Equity Report 2008 – Globalization of Alternative Investments – Working Papers* (ed.by Lerner J. & Gurung A.), vol. 1, Geneva, Switzerland, World Economic Forum, 2008, pp.27- 42.

LERNER J., *Venture Capital and Private Equity – A Casebook*, New York, USA, John Wiley and Sons, 1999.

LEVIN J. S. & ROCAP D. E., *Structuring Venture Capital, Private Equity, and Entrepreneurial Transactions*, New York, USA, Wolters Kluwer Law & Business, 2013.

LJUNGQVIST A. & RICHARDSON M. P., *The Cash Flow, Return and Risk Characteristics of Private Equity*, in *NYU Finance Working Paper*, n. 03-001, 2003.

LJUNGQVIST A., RICHARDSON M. & WOLFENZON D., *The Investment Behavior of Buyout Funds: Theory and Evidence*, in *ECGI – Finance Working Paper*, n. 174, 2007.

LLEWELLY J., *The Business of Climate Change. Challenges and opportunities*, Lehman brothers, October 2007.

LO A. W., *Reading about the Financial Crisis: A Twenty-One-Book Review*, in *Journal of Economic Literature*, vol. 50, n. 1, 2012, pp.151-178.

LOPEZ DE SILANES F., PHALIPPOU L. & GOTTSCHALG O., *Giants at the Gate: On the Cross-Section of Private Equity Investment Returns*, in *EDHEC Working Paper*, 2011.

LUBAROFF M. I. & ALTMAN P. M., *Delaware Limited Partnership*, New York, USA, Aspen Publishers, 2013.

LUCIANO S., *"Cosa sono e perchè vanno molto bene i fondi di private equity,"* in Italia Oggi, n.164, 13/7/2019, p.4.

LUTTER E., *Legal Capital in Europe*, in *European Company and Financial Law Review*, vol. 1, 2006.

MACEY J. R. & ENRIQUES L., *Creditors Versus Capital Formation: The Case Against the European Legal Capital Rules*, in *Cornell Law Review*, vol. 86, 2000-2001, pp.1165-1204.

MACHADO F. S., *Effective Creditor Protection in Private Companies: Mandatory Minimum Capital Rules or Ex Post Mechanisms?*, Mimeo, 2010, available at: http://papers.ssrn.com/sol3/papers.cfm?abstract_id=1568731.

MARASCO F., *"Leveraged" and "Management buy out:" operazioni lecite, operazioni in frode e funzione del notaio*, in *Notariato*, 1996.

MASULIS R. W. & THOMAS R. S., *Does Private Equity Create Wealth? The Effects of Private Equity and Derivatives on Corporate Governance*, in *The University of Chicago Law Review*, vol. 76, 2009, pp.219-260.

MC CAHERY J. A. & VERMEULEN E. P. M., *Recasting Private Equity Funds after the Financial Crisis: The End of 'Two and Twenty' and the Emergence of Co- Investment and Separate Account Arrangements*, in *ECGI – Law Working Paper*, n. 231/2013, 2013.

MC CAHERY J. A. & VERMEULEN E. P. M., *The Contractual Structure and Regulation of Private Equity Funds and Hedge Funds*, in *LSE Working Paper*, n. 50/2008, 2008, available at: http://www.lse.ac.uk/fmg/research/RICAFE/pdf/RICAFE2-WP50McCahery.pdf.

METRICK A. & YASUDA A., *The Economics of Private Equity Funds*, in *Review of Financial Studies*, vol. 23, 2010, pp.2303-2341.

MHETA V., *Principal-Agent Issues in Private Equity and Venture Capital*, in *Wharton Research Scholars Journal*, 2004.

MISHAN E.J., "*Cost-Benefit Analysis: An Introduction,*" New York, USA, Praeger Publishers, 1971.

MONTALENTI P., *Il leveraged buy-out*, Milan, Italy, Giuffrè, 1991.

MONTALENTI P., voce *Leveraged buyout*, in *Enc. Giur. Treccani*, XXIII, Rome, 1999.

MULLINS F., *"Joint Implementation Institutions: Implementing IJ at the National Level,"* Paris, OECD, 2002.

MYERS S. C., *Determinants of Corporate Borrowing*, in *Journal of Financial Economics*, vol. 5, n. 2, 1977, pp.147-175.

NABILOU H., *The Alternative Investment Fund Managers Directive and Hedge Funds' Systemic Risk Regulation in the EU*, 2013.

NAIDECH S. W., *Private Equity Fund Formation*, New York, USA, Practical Law Company, 2011.

NARDI S., *Il leveraged buy out*, in *I nuovi contratti finanziari* (ed.by E. Damiani), Naples, Italy, Edizioni Scientifiche Italiane, 2008.

NEVITT P., *"Project Financing"*, Euromoney, 2000.

NIKOSKELAINEN E. & WRIGHT M., *The impact of corporate governance mechanisms on value increase in leveraged buyouts*, in *Journal of Corporate Finance*, vol. 13, n. 4, 2007, pp.511-537.

OLSON M., *The Logic of Collective Actions: Public Goods and the Theory of Groups*, Cambridge, USA, Harvard University Press, 1965.

OPLER T. C., *Operating performance in leveraged buy-outs*, in *Financial Management*, vol. 21, 1992, pp.27-34.

OUDEJANS L., *Report on the 2016 U.S. Environmental Protection Agency (EPA) International Decontamination Research and Development Conference*. U.S. Environmental Protection Agency, Washington, DC, EPA/600/R-17/174, 2017.

PARDOLESI R., *Leveraged Buyout: una novità a tinte forti (o fosche)?*, in *Giur. comm.*, vol. 3, 1989, pp.402-418.

PAYNE J, *Private equity and its regulation in Europe*, in *Oxford Legal Research Paper Series*, Paper n. 40/2011, 2011, available at: http://papers.ssrn.com/sol3/papers.cfm?abstract_id=1886186.

PERSAUD A. & ATKINSON A., *Private Equity Funds: Legal Analysis of Structural, ERISA, Securities and Other Regulatory Issues*, in *Investment Adviser Regulation* (ed.by Kirsch E. K.), New York, USA, Practising Law Institute, 2012, 47-1, pp.47-66.

PHALIPPOU L., *Beware of Venturing into Private Equity*, in *Journal of Economic Perspectives*, vol. 23, n. 1, 2009, pp.147-166.

POPOV A. & ROOSENBOOM P., *Does private equity investment spur innovation? Evidence from Europe*, in *European Central Bank Working Paper Series*, n. 1063, 2009, available at: http://www.ecb.europa.eu/pub/pdf/scpwps/ecbwp1063.pdf.

POPOV A. & ROOSENBOOM P., *On the real effects of private equity investment – Evidence from business creation*, in *European Central Bank Working Paper Series*, n.1078, 2009,available at: http://www.ecb.europa.eu/pub/pdf/scpwps/ecbwp1078.pdf.

PORTER, M. "*American's green strategy*," Sci. Amer., Apr.1991, p.168.

PREQIN, *2013 Preqin Investor Network Global Alternatives Report Fund Terms and Conditions*, New York, USA, Preqin Investor Network, 2013, available at: https:// www.preqin.com / item / 2013-preqin-investor-network-global-alternativesreport/1/ 6666.

PREQIN, *The 2014 Preqin Global Private Equity Report – Assets Under Management, Dry Powder, Employment and Compensation*, New York, USA, Preqin Investor Network, 2014.

PROBITAS PARTNERS, *"Investing in Infrastructure Funds,"* September 2007.

REINHART C. M. & ROGOFF K. S., *This time it's different: eight centuries of financial folly*, Princeton, USA, Princeton University Press, 2009.

RENNEBOOG L.D.R., SIMONS T. & WRIGHT M., *Why do public firms go private in the UK?*, in Journal of Corporate Finance, vol. 13, n. 4, 2007, pp.591-628.

ROCK E. B., *Adapting to the New Shareholder-Centric Reality*, in *University of Pennsylvania Law Review*, vol. 161, 2013, pp.1907-1988.

ROE M., *Structural Corporate Degradation Due to Too-Big-to-Fail Finance*, in *University of Pennsylvania Law Review*, vol. 162, 2014, pp.1419-1464.

ROMANO R., *Further Assessment of the Iron Law of Financial Regulation: A Postscript to Regulating in the Dark*, in *Yale Law & Economics Research Paper*, n. 515, 2014, available at: http://papers.ssrn.com/sol3/papers.cfm?abstract_id=2517853.

ROMANO R., *Regulating in the Dark*, in *Yale Law & Economics Research Paper*, n. 442, 2012, available at: http://papers.ssrn.com/sol3/papers.cfm?abstract_id=1974148.

ROUBINI N. & MIHM S., *Crisis economics: A crash course in the future of finance*, New York, USA, Penguin Press, 2010.

SAHLMAN W. A., *The Structure and Governance of Venture Capital Organization*, in *Journal of Financial Economics*, vol. 27, 1990, pp.473-521.

SALAFIA V., *Il leveraged buy out nella riforma societaria*, in *Società*, vol. 8, 2004, pp. 935-937.

SBREALEY S., MYER R.A., SANDRI A.F., *Principi di finanza aziendale*, McGraw-Hill, 1999.

SCHELL J., *Private Equity Funds. Business Structure and Operations*, New York, USA, Law Journal Press, 2006.

SCHLESINGER P., *Merger leveraged buy out e riforma societaria*, in *Corr. giur.*, vol. 6, 2003, pp.705-706.

SCHRODERS, *Global Investor Study 2017. Investor behaviour: from priorities to expectations,* 2018.

SERETAKIS A., *A comparative examination of private equity in the United States and Europe: accounting for the past and predicting the future*, in *Fordham Journal of Corporate & Financial Law*, vol. XVIII, 2013, pp.613-668.

SHIVDASANI A. & WANG Y., *Did Structured Credit Fuel the LBO Boom?*, in *The Journal of Finance*, vol. 66, n. 4, 2011, pp.1291-1328.

SMART S. B. & WALDFOGEL J., *Measuring the effect of restructuring on corporate performance: the case of management buy-outs*, in *Review of Economics and Statistics*, vol. 76, 1994, pp.503-511.

SMITH A. J., *Capital ownership structure and performance: the case of management buy-outs*, in *Journal of Financial Economics*, vol. 13, 1990, pp.143-165.

SMITH A., *Wealth of Nations*, Washington, USA, Thrifty Books, 2009.

SPINDLER J. C., *How Private Is Private Equity, and at What Cost?*, in *The University of Chicago Law Review*, vol. 76, 2009, pp.309-332.

SPOLIDORO M. S., voce *Capitale sociale*, in *Enciclopedia del diritto*, IV aggiornamento, Milan, Italy, Giuffrè, 2000.

STEINDL M., *The Alignment of Interest between the General and the Limited Partner in a Private Equity Fund – the Ultimate Governance Nut to Crack?*, in *The Harvard Law School Forum on Corporate Governance and Financial Regulation*,2013, available at: http://blogs.law.harvard.edu/corpgov/tag/martin-steindl/

STERN N., "*The Economics of Climate Change*," Cambridge University Press, March 2014 (online publication).

STRÖMBERG P., *The new demography of private equity*, in *The Global Impact of Private Equity Report 2008 – Globalization of Alternative Investments – Working Papers* (ed.by Lerner J. & Gurung A.), vol. 1, Geneva, Switzerland, World Economic Forum, 2008, pp.3-26.

SUDARSANAM S., WRIGHT M. & HUANG J., *Target bankruptcy audits impact ongoing private performance and exit*, in *Corporate Governance – An International Review*, vol. 19, n. 3, 2011, pp.240-258.

SZEGO B., *Finanziarie l'innovazione: il venture capital dopo la riforma del diritto societario*, in *Rivista del diritto commerciale e del diritto generale delle obbligazioni*, vol. I, 2005, pp.821-866.

SZEGO B., *Il venture capital come strumento per lo sviluppo delle piccole e medie imprese: un'analisi di adeguatezza dell'ordinamento italiano*, in *Banca d'Italia– Quaderni di ricerca giuridica della Consulenza legale*, n. 55, 2002.

SZMIGIERA M., *Private equity-Statistics & Facts,* Statista, 2019.

THALER R. H., *Toward a Positive Theory of Consumer Choice*, in *Journal of Economic Behavior and Organization,* vol. 1, 2008, pp.39-60.

THORNTON P., *Inside the Dark Box: Shedding Light on Private Equity*, London, UK, The Work Foundation, 2007.

TIROLE J., *The Theory of Corporate Finance*, Princeton, USA, Princeton University Press, 2006.

UGHETTO E., *Assessing the contribution to innovation of private equity investors: a study on European buyouts*, in *Research Policy*, vol. 39, 2010, pp.126-140.

UN, *United Nations Conference on Environment and Development (UNCED)*, Earth Summit, 1992, available at:https://sustainabledevelopment.un.org/milestones/unced.

VON DRATHEN C. & FALEIRO F., *The performance of leveraged buy-out-backed IPOs in the UK*, in *London Business School Working Paper*, 2007, available at: http://papers.ssrn.com/sol3/papers.cfm?abstract_id=1117185.

WALKER, S.T., *Understanding Alternative Investments: Creating Diversified portfolios that ride the wave of investment success,* New York, USA, Palgrave Macmillan, 2014.

WEIR C., JONES P. & WRIGHT M., *Public to Private Transactions, Private Equity and Performance in the UK: An Empirical Analysis of the Impact of Going Private*, in *Nottingham University Business School Research Paper*, 2008, available at: http://papers.ssrn.com/sol3/papers.cfm?abstract_id=113 8616.

WHITEHEAD C. K., *The Evolution of Debt; Covenants, the Credit Market, and Corporate Governance*, in *The Journal of Corporation Law*, vol. 34, n. 3, 2009, pp.641-677.

WILSON N. & WRIGHT M., *Private Equity, Buy-Outs and Insolvency Risk*, in *Journal of Business Finance & Accounting*, vol. 40, n. 7-8, 2013, pp.949-990.

WILSON N., WRIGHT M., SIEGEL D. & SCHOLES, L., *Private equity portfolio company performance during the global recession*, in *Journal of Corporate Finance*, vol. 18, n. 1, 2012, pp.193-205.

WILSON, J. W., *The New Venturers – Inside the High-Stakes World of Venture Capital*, Beverly, USA, Addison Wesley Publishing Company, 1986.

WORLD BANK, *Climate Finance*, 4 October 2019.

WORLD BANK REPORT, *State and trends of the carbon market 2011*, Washington DC, n.63270, 2011.

WORLD BANK REPORT, *State and Trends of the Carbon Market 2012*, Washington DC, n.76837, 2012.

WORLD ENERGY OUTLOOK 2019, available at: https://www.iea.org/reports/world-energy-outlook-2019.

WRIGHT M., BURROWS A., BALL R., SCHOLES L., MEULEMAN M. & AMESS K., *The Implications of Alternative Investment Vehicles for Corporate Governance (Report prepared for the Steering Group on Corporate Governance)*, Paris, France, OECD, 2007.

WRIGHT M., JELIC R. & SAADOUNI B., *Performance of Private to Public MBOs: The Role of Venture Capital*, in *Journal of Business Finance & Accounting*, vol. 32, n. 3-4, 2005, pp.643-682.

WSO, *Overview of Infrastructure Private Equity,* 2 January 2017.

YESCOMBE E.R., *Principles of Project Finance*, Academic Press, 2002.

ZETSCHE D.A., *The AIFM Directive 2011/61/EU European Regulation of Alternative Investment Funds*, New York, USA, Kluwer Law International, 2013.

www.ingramcontent.com/pod-product-compliance
Lightning Source LLC
LaVergne TN
LVHW010621300926
849162LV00001B/26
* 9 7 8 1 6 8 0 5 3 0 9 4 0 *